Current
CONTROVERSIES

Immigration, Asylum, and Sanctuary Cities

Other Books in the Current Controversies Series

Immigration, Asylum, and Sanctuary Cities

Ariana Agrios, Book Editor

GREENHAVEN
PUBLISHING

Published in 2021 by Greenhaven Publishing, LLC
353 3rd Avenue, Suite 255, New York, NY 10010

Articles in Greenhaven Publishing anthologies are often edited for length to meet page
requirements. In addition, original titles of these works are changed to clearly present
the main thesis and to explicitly indicate the author's opinion. Every effort is made to
ensure that Greenhaven Publishing accurately reflects the original intent of the authors.
Every effort has been made to trace the owners of the copyrighted material.

Cover image: Procyk Radek/Shutterstock.com

Library of Congress Cataloging-in-Publication Data

Names: Agrios, Ariana, editor.
Title: Immigration, asylum, and sanctuary cities / Ariana Agrios, book
    editor.
Description: First edition. | New York : Greenhaven Publishing, 2021. |
    Series: Current controversies | Includes bibliographical references and
    index. | Audience: Grades 9–12.
Identifiers: LCCN 2019057339 | ISBN 9781534507098 (library binding) | ISBN
    9781534507081 (paperback)
Subjects: LCSH: United States—Emigration and immigration—Government
    policy—Juvenile literature. | United States—Emigration and
    immigration—Social aspects—Juvenile literature. | Illegal
    aliens—United States—Juvenile literature. | Cities and towns—United
    States—Juvenile literature.
Classification: LCC JV6483 .I55364 2021 | DDC 325.73—dc23
LC record available at https://lccn.loc.gov/2019057339

Manufactured in the United States of America

Website: http://greenhavenpublishing.com

Contents

Chapter 2: Do Sanctuary Cities Pose a Threat to Security and Well-Being?

Yes: Sanctuary Cities and Immigration Pose a Threat to Security and Well-Being

By threatening to remove federal funding from sanctuary cities, President Trump opens the door for increased crime, as law enforcement will have fewer resources to help fight it.

Jeff Proctor

By adhering to sanctuary city protocol, police are sometimes forced into ineffective and inefficient public safety tactics.

No: Sanctuary Cities Are Not a Threat to Public Safety

America's Voice Education Fund

Sanctuary cities follow federal and constitutional law by protecting individual rights and treating immigration as a civil—not criminal—violation.

Raul Reyes

Sanctuary cities actually serve to make communities safer, as they allow illegal immigrants to feel comfortable communicating with law enforcement without fear of deportation.

Chuck Wexler

Many police chiefs support sanctuary cities since they enable them to do their jobs more effectively, communicate with constituents, and keep crime down.

Chapter 3: Are Countries Obligated to Allow Legal Residence?

Obed Manuel and Brianna Stone

Differences in the circumstances under which immigrants enter the United States dictate the laws to which they are subject. This viewpoint provides an overview of these various circumstances.

Yes: Immigrants and Asylum Seekers Have a Right to Legal Residence

Chapter 4: Are Countries Culturally Improved by Immigration?

Foreword

"Controversy" is a word that has an undeniably unpleasant connotation. It carries a definite negative charge. Controversy can spoil family gatherings, spread a chill around classroom and campus discussion, inflame public discourse, open raw civic wounds, and lead to the ouster of public officials. We often feel that controversy is almost akin to bad manners, a rude and shocking eruption of that which must not be spoken or thought of in polite, tightly guarded society. To avoid controversy, to quell controversy, is often seen as a public good, a victory for etiquette, perhaps even a moral or ethical imperative.

Yet the studious, deliberate avoidance of controversy is also a whitewashing, a denial, a death threat to democracy. It is a false sterilizing and sanitizing and superficial ordering of the messy, ragged, chaotic, at times ugly processes by which a healthy democracy identifies and confronts challenges, engages in passionate debate about appropriate approaches and solutions, and arrives at something like a consensus and a broadly accepted and supported way forward. Controversy is the megaphone, the speaker's corner, the public square through which the citizenry finds and uses its voice. Controversy is the life's blood of our democracy and absolutely essential to the vibrant health of our society.

Our present age is certainly no stranger to controversy. We are consumed by fierce debates about technology, privacy, political correctness, poverty, violence, crime and policing, guns, immigration, civil and human rights, terrorism, militarism, environmental protection, and gender and racial equality. Loudly competing voices are raised every day, shouting opposing opinions, putting forth competing agendas, and summoning starkly different visions of a utopian or dystopian future. Often these voices attempt to shout the others down; there is precious little listening and considering among the cacophonous din. Yet listening and considering, too, are essential to the health of a democracy. If controversy is democracy's lusty lifeblood, respectful listening and careful thought are its higher faculties, its brain, its conscience.

Current Controversies does not shy away from or attempt to hush the loudly competing voices. It seeks to provide readers with as wide and representative as possible a range of articulate voices on any given controversy of the day, separates each one out to allow it to be heard clearly and fairly, and encourages careful listening to each of these well-crafted, thoughtfully expressed opinions, supplied by some of today's leading academics, thinkers, analysts, politicians, policy makers, economists, activists, change agents, and advocates. Only after listening to a wide range of opinions on an issue, evaluating the strengths and weaknesses of each argument, assessing how well the facts and available evidence mesh with the stated opinions and conclusions, and thoughtfully and critically examining one's own beliefs and conscience can the reader begin to arrive at his or her own conclusions and articulate his or her own stance on the spotlighted controversy.

This process is facilitated and supported in each Current Controversies volume by an introduction and chapter overviews that provide readers with the essential context they need to begin engaging with the spotlighted controversies, with the debates surrounding them, and with their own perhaps shifting or nascent opinions on them. Chapters are organized around several key questions that are answered with diverse opinions representing all points on the political spectrum. In its content, organization, and methodology, readers are encouraged to determine the authors' point of view and purpose, interrogate and analyze the various arguments and their rhetoric and structure, evaluate the arguments' strengths and weaknesses, test their claims against available facts and evidence, judge the validity of the reasoning, and bring into clearer, sharper focus the reader's own beliefs and conclusions and how they may differ from or align with those in the collection or those of classmates.

Research has shown that reading comprehension skills improve dramatically when students are provided with compelling, intriguing, and relevant "discussable" texts. The subject matter of these collections could not be more compelling, intriguing, or urgently relevant to today's students and the world they are poised to inherit. The anthologized articles also provide the basis for stimulating, lively, and passionate classroom debates. Students who are compelled to anticipate objections to their own argument and identify the flaws in those of an opponent read more carefully, think more critically, and steep themselves in relevant context, facts, and information more thoroughly. In short, using discussable text of the kind provided by every single volume in the Current Controversies series encourages close reading, facilitates reading comprehension, fosters research, strengthens critical thinking, and greatly enlivens and energizes classroom discussion and participation. The entire learning process is deepened, extended, and strengthened.

If we are to foster a knowledgeable, responsible, active, and engaged citizenry, we must provide readers with the intellectual, interpretive, and critical-thinking tools and experience necessary to make sense of the world around them and of the all-important debates and arguments that inform it. We must encourage them not to run away from or attempt to quell controversy but to embrace it in a responsible, conscientious, and thoughtful way, to sharpen and strengthen their own informed opinions by listening to and critically analyzing those of others. This series encourages respectful engagement with and analysis of current controversies and competing opinions and fosters a resulting increase in the strength and rigor of one's own opinions and stances. As such, it helps readers assume their rightful place in the public square and provides them with the skills necessary to uphold their awesome responsibility—guaranteeing the continued and future health of a vital, vibrant, and free democracy.

Introduction

> *"America was indebted to immigration for her settlement and prosperity. That part of America which had encouraged them most had advanced most rapidly in population, agriculture and the arts."*
>
> —James Madison, Founding Father and fourth president of the United States

Immigration is the process of moving across international borders to live in a new country, either permanently or for an extended period of time. This process is anything but simple. Immigration can be cyclical or temporary; it might occur due to origin country expelling forces or attractive benefits in the host country. People may come fleeing violence, seeking asylum, bringing family, or leaving everything behind. There are thousands of ways and reasons to seek out residency in a new country.

Though perhaps it is cliché to say at this point, America is a nation of immigrants. Many of America's first immigrants took refuge here and hoped the United States would be a place for freedom of religion and speech—a home for those oppressed in other nations. Of course, this dream wasn't available to all. Years passed with stringent immigration restrictions for certain nations and racist quotas that outright limited entry. Though legislation eventually changed these constraints and public opinion shifted, immigration remains a controversial and complicated topic. Stricter border security and an attempted ban of Muslim people (as exemplified by 2017's Executive Order 13769) continue today as America once again tries to guard its borders. In this changing political context the question becomes: How should we regulate international movement?

To answer this question, one needs to understand the broader scope of circumstances driving immigration today and the definitional differences in those forces. This volume focuses on immigration as a whole, but with a particular focus on asylum seekers and sanctuary cities. While immigration can refer to any type of movement across borders, asylum specifically denotes the refuge given to persons fleeing conflict or persecution in their home country. Special attention is often given to asylum seekers. Many countries impose fewer entry restrictions on such persecuted individuals, but these migrants often still face extreme difficulties upon arrival in their host countries. Many leave their homes with nothing and arrive unable to work or receive state benefits due to local policies. In the United States, asylum seekers must prove they face specific persecution on the basis of religion, race, or political beliefs, and often must come directly from that country with no prior respites in other host nations. Gender-based violence and other forms of oppression do not qualify migrants to seek asylum in the US.

Sanctuary cities are also often misunderstood. Rather than a place of refuge specifically for asylum seekers or a community that protects criminals from prosecution, these cities are simply those that state they will not take extra steps to detain illegal immigrants. Police operate as usual in sanctuary cities but refuse to detain anyone simply for being an illegal immigrant. If an illegal immigrant commits a crime, they are still arrested and treated like any other American lawbreaker. However, police will not detain anyone longer than legally acceptable in order to comply with Immigration and Customs Enforcement (ICE) and may not share the illegal status of arrested residents with ICE. These cities assert that their choice is constitutionally protected, but the decision to disobey federal law has led to many conflicts between local and federal leaders and subsequent court cases.

Given the range of international pressures and conflicts, opening US borders can seem ethically essential. But reality poses significant problems that force citizens and politicians to consider how to regulate migration. The United States is working with a finite amount of resources and must decide how much to allocate to immigration-related issues. This is a problem of priorities and is especially problematic when the economy is lagging and the government has made other service-based commitments to its constituents. Additionally, immigration is tied deeply to national security. While the vast majority of migrants arrive seeking simple freedoms and pursuing the American dream, the US is responsible for monitoring these processes to protect its citizens from any harm foreign actors may attempt to inflict. Logistically, open borders present an imposing number of challenges, which forces the United States to make choices in how it limits immigration—and more specifically, whom it limits.

So if a country must limit whom it admits, what factors should be taken into consideration? Do immigrants contribute economically to their host country? Most studies show positive correlations between immigration and economic growth and prosperity, but are there still some who lose out in these transactions? Do immigrants culturally enrich their country, or does their presence threaten the cultural traditions of host countries? What kind of safety issues does immigration pose, and what kind of obligations do countries have toward those seeking a better life? Do ethical obligations go beyond national borders? *Current Controversies: Immigration, Asylum, and Sanctuary Cities* seeks to explore these ideas and prompt the reader to draw conclusions about immigration and asylum in today's increasingly connected world.

CHAPTER 1

Are Countries Economically Improved by Immigration?

Immigration History and Reform in the US

OpenStax College and Lumen Learning

OpenStax College and Lumen Learning are two partner companies that strive to make educational materials and opportunities freely available in an online framework.

Most Americans would be outraged if a law prevented them from moving to another city or another state. However, when the conversation turns to crossing national borders and are about other people arriving in the United States, laws preventing such movement often seem more reasonable. Some of the tensions over immigration stem from worries over how it might affect a country's culture, including differences in language, and patterns of family, authority, or gender relationships. Economics does not have much to say about such cultural issues. Some of the worries about immigration do, however, have to do with its effects on wages and income levels, and how it affects government taxes and spending. On those topics, economists have insights and research to offer.

Historical Patterns of Immigration

Supporters and opponents of immigration look at the same data and see different patterns. Those who express concern about immigration levels to the United States point to data that shows total inflows of immigrants decade by decade through the twentieth century. Clearly, the level of immigration has been high and rising in recent years, reaching and exceeding the towering levels of the early twentieth century. However, those who are less worried about immigration point out that the high immigration levels of the early twentieth century happened when total population was much lower. Since the U.S. population roughly tripled during the

"Microeconomics: Immigration," by OpenStax College, Lumen Learning, https://courses.lumenlearning.com/wmopen-microeconomics/chapter/immigration/. Licensed under CC BY 4.0 International.

twentieth century, the seemingly high levels in immigration in the 1990s and 2000s look relatively smaller when they are divided by the population.

From where have the immigrants come? Immigrants from Europe were more than 90% of the total in the first decade of the twentieth century, but less than 20% of the total by the end of the century. By the 2000s, about half of U.S. immigration came from the rest of the Americas, especially Mexico, and about a quarter came from various countries in Asia.

Economic Effects of Immigration

A surge of immigration can affect the economy in a number of different ways. In this section, we will consider how immigrants might benefit the rest of the economy, how they might affect wage levels, and how they might affect government spending at the federal and local level.

To understand the economic consequences of immigration, consider the following scenario. Imagine that the immigrants entering the United States matched the existing U.S. population in age range, education, skill levels, family size, and occupations. How would immigration of this type affect the rest of the U.S. economy? Immigrants themselves would be much better off, because their standard of living would be higher in the United States. Immigrants would contribute to both increased production and increased consumption. Given enough time for adjustment, the range of jobs performed, income earned, taxes paid, and public services needed would not be much affected by this kind of immigration. It would be as if the population simply increased a little.

Now, consider the reality of recent immigration to the United States. Immigrants are not identical to the rest of the U.S. population. About one-third of immigrants over the age of 25 lack a high school diploma. As a result, many of the recent immigrants end up in jobs like restaurant and hotel work, lawn care, and janitorial work. This kind of immigration represents a shift to the right in the supply of unskilled labor for a number of jobs, which will lead to lower wages for these jobs. The middle- and upper-income households that purchase the services of these unskilled workers will benefit from these lower wages. However, low-skilled U.S. workers who must compete with low-skilled immigrants for jobs will tend to suffer from immigration.

The difficult policy questions about immigration are not so much about the overall gains to the rest of the economy, which seem to be real but small in the context of the U.S. economy, as they are about the disruptive effects of immigration in specific labor markets. One disruptive effect, as we noted, is that immigration weighted toward low-skill workers tends to reduce wages for domestic low-skill workers. A study by Michael S. Clune found that for each 10% rise in the number of employed immigrants with no more than a high school diploma in the labor market, high school students reduced their annual number of hours worked by 3%. The effects on wages of low-skill workers are not large—perhaps in the range of decline of about 1%. These effects are likely kept low, in part, because of the legal floor of federal and state minimum wage laws. In addition, immigrants are also thought to contribute to increased demand for local goods and services which can stimulate the local low skilled labor market. It is also possible that employers, in the face of abundant low-skill workers may choose production processes which are more labor intensive than otherwise would have been. These various factors would explain the small negative wage effect that the native low-skill workers observed as a result of immigration.

Another potential disruptive effect is the impact on state and local government budgets. Many of the costs imposed by immigrants are costs that arise in state-run programs, like the cost of public schooling and of welfare benefits. However, many of the taxes that immigrants pay are federal taxes like income taxes and Social Security taxes. Many immigrants do not own property (such as homes and cars), so they do not pay property taxes, which are one of the main sources of state and local tax revenue. However, they do pay sales taxes, which are state and local, and the landlords of property they rent pay property taxes. According to the nonprofit Rand Corporation, the effects of immigration on taxes are generally positive at the federal level, but they are negative at the state and local levels in places where there are many low-skilled immigrants.

Proposals for Immigration Reform

The Congressional Jordan Commission of the 1990s proposed reducing overall levels of immigration and refocusing U.S. immigration policy to give priority to immigrants with higher skill levels. In the labor market, focusing on high-skilled immigrants would help prevent any negative effects on low-skilled workers' wages. For government budgets, higher-skilled workers find jobs more quickly, earn higher wages, and pay more in taxes. Several other immigration-friendly countries, notably Canada and Australia, have immigration systems where those with high levels of education or job skills have a much better chance of obtaining permission to immigrate. For the United States, high tech companies regularly ask for a more lenient immigration policy to admit a greater quantity of highly skilled workers under the H1B visa program.

The Obama Administration proposed the so-called "DREAM Act" legislation, which would have offered a path to citizenship for illegal immigrants brought to the United States before the age of 16. Despite bipartisan support, the legislation failed to pass at the federal level. However, some state legislatures, such as California, have passed their own Dream Acts.

Between its plans for a border wall, increased deportation of undocumented immigrants, and even reductions in the number of highly skilled legal H1B immigrants, the Trump Administration has a much less positive approach to immigration. Most economists, whether conservative or liberal, believe that while immigration harms some domestic workers, the benefits to the nation exceed the costs. However, given the Trump Administration's opposition, any significant immigration reform is likely on hold.

Immigration and a Stronger Workforce

Wharton School of the University of Pennsylvania

The Wharton School of the University of Pennsylvania is one of the leading business schools in the United States, focusing on education and innovative ways to drive economic growth and improve business practices.

Today, the United States is home to the largest immigrant population in the world. Even though immigrants assimilate faster in the United States compared to developed European nations, immigration policy has become a highly contentious issue in America. While much of the debate centers on cultural issues, the economic effects of immigration are clear: Economic analysis finds little support for the view that inflows of foreign labor have reduced jobs or Americans' wages. Economic theory predictions and the bulk of academic research confirms that wages are unaffected by immigration over the long-term and that the economic effects of immigration are mostly positive for natives and for the overall economy.

The foreign-born population has grown rapidly in recent decades, rising from less than 5 percent of the U.S. population in 1970 to 13 percent in 2013. Although immigrants today comprise a larger share of the population than at any time since World War II, the foreign-born share today is roughly the same as during the late 19th and early 20th centuries, when about 15 percent of U.S. residents were born in a foreign country.

Has the surge in immigration since 1970 led to slower wage growth for native-born workers? Academic research does not provide much support for this claim. The evidence suggests that when immigration increases the supply of labor, firms increase investment to offset any reduction in capital per worker, thereby

"The Effects of Immigration on the United States' Economy," Wharton School of the University of Pennsylvania, June 27, 2016, Knowledge@Wharton (https://knowledge.wharton.upenn.edu/). Reprinted by permission.

keeping average wages from falling over the long term. Moreover, immigrants are often imperfect substitutes for native-born workers in U.S. labor markets. That means they do not compete for the same jobs and put minimal downward pressure on natives' wages. This might explain why competition from new immigrants has mostly affected earlier immigrants, who experienced significant reductions in wages from the surge in immigration. In contrast, studies find that immigration has actually raised average wages of native-born workers during the last few decades.

Immigrants are at the forefront of innovation and ingenuity in the United States, accounting for a disproportionately high share of patent filings, science and technology graduates, and senior positions at top venture capital-funded firms. In addition, the presence of immigrants often creates opportunities for less-skilled native workers to become more specialized in their work, thereby increasing their productivity.

Immigration generally also improves the government's fiscal situation, as many immigrants pay more in taxes over a lifetime than they consume in government services. However, native-born residents of states with large concentrations of less-educated immigrants may face larger tax burdens, as these immigrants pay less in taxes and are more likely to send children to public schools.

Labor Market Competition

A popular view is that immigrants are taking jobs from American citizens. However, although immigrants increase the supply of labor, they also spend their wages on homes, food, TVs and other goods and services and expand domestic economic demand. This increased demand, in turn, generates more jobs to build those homes, make and sell food, and transport TVs.

Most empirical studies indicate long-term benefits for natives' employment and wages from immigration, although some studies suggest that these gains come at the cost of short-term losses from lower wages and higher unemployment.

Standard economic theory implies that while higher labor supply from immigration may initially depress wages, over time firms increase investment to restore the amount of capital per worker, which then restores wages. Steady growth in the capital-labor ratio prevents workers' average productivity, and therefore their average wages from declining over the long run. The data shows the pre-1980 trend in the capital-labor ratio extrapolated over the next few decades—the period when U.S. immigration accelerated. Consistent with the theory, the actual capital-labor ratio did not significantly or permanently deviate from that trend after 1980.

While growth in the capital stock keeps average wages from falling, immigration may affect the relative wages of different types of workers by changing their relative supplies. Immigration over the last few decades has had a bimodal impact across education groups: The largest impact has been on the supply of workers without a high school degree and of workers at the high end of the education spectrum—those with a college or postgraduate degree. Relative to the native-born, recently-arrived immigrants are less likely to have completed high school. At the same time, at the higher end, recent immigrants are more likely to have completed college and hold advanced degrees than their native counterparts. Thus, immigration has primarily raised the supplies of the least and the most skilled workers.

Despite these increases in labor supply, in many cases immigrants appear to complement American-born workers rather than replacing them. Because less-educated immigrants often lack the linguistic skills required for many jobs, they tend to take jobs in manual labor-intensive occupations such as agriculture and construction. Even for low-skilled native-born workers in these industries, the effects of increased competition from immigrants are ambiguous, as many take advantage of their superior communication abilities and shift into occupations where these skills are more valuable, such as personal services and sales.

Similarly, highly educated immigrants face a disadvantage in communication-intensive jobs, and therefore tend to work in scientific and technical occupations. Highly skilled natives in management, media, and other culture- and language-dependent jobs face little competition from high skilled immigrants. The inflow of foreign labor is, therefore, concentrated in a subset of occupations that tend to employ many immigrants already. Consequently, it is earlier immigrants who face the greatest increase in competitive pressure.

Two academic analyses of the wage impacts of immigration over the last several decades account for firms' investment response and the imperfect substitutability between immigrant and native-born workers. They find a small but positive effect, equal to about half a percentage point, on the average wages of native workers. One of the studies indicates a minor decline in the wages of those without a high school degree or with a college degree, while the other study finds only positive gains. In sharp contrast, both studies find that earlier immigrants experienced wage declines, on average, of 4 to 7 percent concentrated among the most and least educated.

Productivity

Immigrants also bring a wave of talent and ingenuity, accounting for a disproportionate share of workers in the fields most closely tied with innovation. A 2011 survey of the top fifty venture capital funded companies found that half had at least one immigrant founder and three quarters had immigrants in top management or research positions. A significant share of advanced degrees awarded in science and engineering—often the foundation for innovation and job growth—go to foreign-born students with temporary visas studying in American universities. According to a 2012 National Science Board report, foreign students earned 27 percent of science and engineering master's degrees in 2009. And in recent years, the number of foreign-born undergraduate students studying in American universities has grown rapidly, rising to 18 percent between 2011 and 2012.

In 2011, 76 percent of patents from top 10 U.S. patent-producing universities had at least one foreign-born author. Indeed, immigrants produce patents at double the rate as natives, and the presence of these immigrants generates positive spillovers on patenting by natives. Economic theory suggests a direct link between a skilled and innovative labor force and faster GDP growth, and more than three quarters of U.S. growth over the last 150 years can be explained by improvements in education and research-driven innovation.

Moreover, states with a high concentration of foreign-born workers experience significantly faster productivity growth. As discussed earlier, less-skilled natives often respond to increased competition from immigrants by leaving manual labor for occupations that emphasize language and communication skills. This greater specialization leads to a more efficient allocation of labor, raising the incomes and productivity of both natives and immigrants.

Fiscal Impact

Immigrants in general — whether documented or undocumented —are net positive contributors to the federal budget. However, the fiscal impact varies widely at the state and local levels and is contingent on the characteristics of the immigrant population—age, education, and skill level—living within each state.

Immigrants, and especially recent arrivals, are generally of working age; thus, they impose relatively small costs on Social Security and Medicare—the largest components of federal non-defense spending. While immigrants' taxes help pay for defense spending, they do not generate any additional significant costs for the military, thereby somewhat reducing the federal tax burden of the average native.

More often than not, immigrants are less educated and their incomes are lower at all ages than those of natives. As a result, immigrants pay less in federal, state, and local taxes and use federally-funded entitlement programs such as Medicaid, SNAP, and other benefits at higher rates than natives. But they are also less likely than comparably low income natives to receive public assistance. Moreover, when they do take public assistance, the average value of benefits received is below average, implying a smaller net cost to the federal government relative to a comparable low income native.

However, immigrants often impose a heavier tax burden on natives at the state and local level. Immigrants—particularly those with low levels of education and income—generally have larger families and more children using public K-12 education, the largest component of state and local budgets. Furthermore, if immigrants' children are not already fluent English speakers, the per-student cost of education may be substantially higher than for native-born children. These factors impose short-term costs on state budgets. Over the long term, however, the upward economic mobility and taxpaying lifetime of second generation immigrants more than offset the initial fiscal burden.

Because the net cost to state and local governments is closely related to immigrants' education and income, the socioeconomic composition of the immigrant population determines the fiscal impact in each state. For example, because New Jersey has a high proportion of well-educated and high income immigrants who contribute more to state and local revenues than they consume in public services, the net fiscal burden of immigration is small in New Jersey. In contrast, California's high share of less-educated and low-income immigrants means that immigrants' contribution to state and local revenues is smaller relative to their consumption of public services. As a result, the estimated fiscal burden of immigration is five times higher for native residents of California than of New Jersey.

Conclusion

Economists generally agree that the effects of immigration on the U.S. economy are broadly positive. Immigrants, whether high- or low-skilled, legal or illegal, are unlikely to replace native-born workers or reduce their wages over the long-term, though they may cause some short-term dislocations in labor markets. Indeed, the experience of the last few decades suggests that immigration may actually have significant long-term benefits for the native-born, pushing them into higher-paying occupations and raising the overall pace of innovation and productivity growth. Moreover, as baby boomers have begun moving into retirement in advanced economies around the world, immigration is helping to keep America comparatively young and reducing the burden of financing retirement benefits for a growing elderly population. While natives bear some upfront costs for the provision of public services to immigrants and their families, the evidence suggests a net positive return on the investment over the long term.

Immigrants Fill Necessary Gaps in the Labor Market

Brennan Hoban

Brennan Hoban is a writer and communications manager at the Brookings Institution.

Throughout his campaign and into his presidency, President Trump has promised to implement new immigration policies that will help improve the U.S. economy and job market.

A motivating factor behind Trump's proposed policies—including the construction of a new U.S.-Mexico border wall, more border patrol agents, and stricter deportation policies—is his belief that immigrants are stealing job opportunities from American workers. As he said in July 2015, "They're taking our jobs. They're taking our manufacturing jobs. They're taking our money. They're killing us."

But is that really the case? In new research, Brookings experts explore how immigration affects the economy, and what Trump's proposed policies could mean for the future of the U.S. workforce.

Trump's Proposed Policies Aim to Decrease Immigration

In one of his first proactive attempts to decrease the number of immigrants illegally entering the U.S. and the nation's workforce, Trump has vowed to increase the number of U.S. Border Patrol Agents to an unprecedented 26,370.

Trump has also proposed building a wall along the U.S. Mexico border in order to prevent immigration into the U.S. This border wall has been a priority for President Trump since his campaign. At a recent campaign rally in Arizona, Trump threatened to shut

"Do immigrants 'steal' jobs from American workers?" by Brennan Hoban, The Brookings Institution, August 24, 2017. Reprinted by permission.

down the government if Congress does not allocate funding to building a border wall.

Immigrants Often Fill the Jobs Americans Don't Want

However, some argue that the work of these agents to protect against "job-stealing" immigrants may be in vain. As Brookings Senior Fellow Vanda Felbab-Brown explains in her new Brookings Essay, "The Wall," immigrants may not actually be "stealing" as many U.S. jobs as Trump thinks. As she put it, "the impact of immigrant labor on the wages of native-born workers is low… However, undocumented workers often work the unpleasant, back-breaking jobs that native-born workers are not willing to do."

Felbab-Brown explains that many of the jobs occupied by undocumented workers in the United States are physically demanding jobs that Americans do not want, such as gutting fish or work on farm fields. She argues, "fixing immigration is not about mass deportations of people but about creating a legal visa system for jobs Americans do not want. And it is about providing better education opportunities, skills-development and retooling, and safety nets for American workers. And to date, Trump hasn't offered serious policy proposals on many—if any—of these areas."

Prioritizing Only High-Skilled Immigrants Isn't Necessary

But what about *legal* immigrants and high-skilled workers? Brookings Senior Fellow William Frey takes issue with a proposal from President Trump to cut quotas for legal immigration in half and to prioritize the entrance of those with high skills. He argues that "these [proposals] fly in the face of census statistics that show that current immigration levels are increasingly vital to the growth of much of America, and that recent arrivals are more highly skilled than ever before."

As for prioritizing immigrants with high skill levels, Frey points out that recent immigrants are already more highly educated than those of the past. In fact, he explains that "college graduates are more prevalent among recent immigrant adults than among all adults in 90 of the 100 largest metropolitan areas."

Immigration Is Tied to Positive Economic Growth and Innovation

Frey also explains that immigration is especially important for areas that are experiencing a decline in domestic migration and that U.S. immigration levels are currently fueling most community demographic gains. These gains are especially important as the nation's population gets older and fertility remains low.

Brookings Senior Fellow Dany Bahar also examined the positive link between immigration and economic growth. Bahar explains that while immigrants represent about 15 percent of the general U.S. workforce, they account for around a quarter of entrepreneurs and a quarter of investors in the U.S. and that over one third of new firms have at least one immigrant entrepreneur in its initial leadership team.

Moreover, Bahar explains that the impact of immigration on the wages of native-born workers is very small. "If anything," he concludes, "negative impacts occur for the most part on wages of prior immigrants with similar set of skills."

As Bahar mentions, "by cutting on immigration, the country will miss an opportunity for new inventions and ventures that could generate the jobs that the president is so committed to bring back. Thus, if the current administration wants to create jobs and 'make America great again,' it should consider enlisting more migrants."

Immigration Is Not the Cause of Unemployment in the US

Amita Kelly

Amita Kelly is a national desk senior digital editor at NPR. She previously worked as a digital editor for the Washington desk and covered politics and government proceedings.

President Trump's senior policy adviser Stephen Miller had a tense exchange with reporters at Wednesday's press briefing as he defended the administration's new proposal to dramatically curtail legal immigration. The plan prioritizes highly skilled workers over family members for green cards.

The administration reasons that too many low-skilled immigrant workers are entering the country, costing Americans jobs and wages.

Miller said the U.S. has, in recent years, issued green cards without regard to whether an immigrant can "pay their own way or be reliant on welfare, or whether they'll displace or take a job from an American worker."

Calling a green card the "golden ticket" of immigration, Miller said Trump's proposal "puts the needs of the working class ahead of the investor class."

"We're protecting blue-collar workers," he said.

The Claim

"We've seen significant reductions in wages for blue-collar workers, massive displacement of African-American and Hispanic workers, as well as the displacement of immigrant workers from previous years who oftentimes compete directly against new arrivals who are being paid even less," Stephen Miller said.

Miller went on to say the "numbers of low-skilled [immigrant] workers in particular is a major detriment to U.S. workers."

The Question

Have immigrants taken jobs from and lowered wages for American blue-collar workers?

The Short Answer

Economists disagree whether or how much an influx of immigrants depresses wages. Some have found that new immigrants depress wages for certain groups, such as teenagers or workers with a high school diploma or less. Others say the overall effect on the economy is tiny, and an influx of immigrant workers vitalizes the economy overall.

Either way, the forces driving wage reductions for blue-collar workers go far beyond immigration.

The Long Answer

It is true that wages for low-wage workers have declined — they fell 5 percent from 1979 to 2013. That may not seem like a huge drop, but during that same period, the hourly wages of high-wage workers rose 41 percent, according to the Economic Policy Institute.

However, economists disagree over whether an influx of immigrant labor caused or contributed to declining blue-collar jobs and wages.

Asked to provide a study that supported the administration's assertion, Stephen Miller cited work from George Borjas, a Harvard labor economist, on how the Mariel boatlift affected blue-collar wages in Miami. In 1980, 125,000 Cuban immigrants came to the U.S., mostly Miami, from the town of Mariel.

Borjas, Miller said, "went back and re-examined and opened up the old data, and talked about how it actually did reduce wages for workers who were living there at the time."

Borjas' new analysis found that the wages of high school dropouts in Miami dropped between 10-30 percent after the refugee influx (the analysis looked at 1977 to 1993).

But an earlier study on the boatlift, from 1990 by Princeton economist David Card, looked at wages of "less-skilled" workers overall (as opposed to just high school dropouts) and found "virtually no effect on the wages or unemployment rates of less-skilled workers, even among Cubans who had immigrated earlier."

The debate remains unsettled, and it's impossible to extrapolate the effect of the boatlift on Miami to the whole country.

A recent analysis commissioned and published by the National Academies of Sciences, Engineering, and Medicine found "the literature on *employment* impacts finds little evidence that immigration significantly affects the overall employment levels of native-born workers."

Overall, the analysis called the inflow of foreign-born people "a relatively minor factor in the $18 trillion U.S. economy." However, the analysis does cite recent research that immigration could reduce the number of hours worked by teenagers and some evidence that recent immigrants reduce the employment rate of prior immigrants.

There are, of course, other forces that have depressed blue-collar wages: increased automation, globalization, declining unionization and government policies on overtime. The Trump administration recently said it would not defend an Obama-era rule that made workers who make less than $47,000 per year (up from about $24,000) eligible for overtime.

Not Just About Economics

The politics of the bill reach beyond economics. At Wednesday's briefing, Miller was also asked to defend the fact that the bill prioritizes English-speaking immigrants. Miller, along with adviser Steve Bannon, have led an ethnonationalist wing at the White House. Bannon has complained about the number of Asian CEOs in Silicon Valley, implying that they are adversarial to America's "civic society."

"Are we just going to bring in people from Great Britain and Australia?" CNN's Jim Acosta asked.

"The notion that you think this is a racist bill is so wrong and so insulting," Miller answered, adding that the country's foreign-born population into the U.S. "has quadrupled since 1970."

While Miller is correct that the foreign-born population has increased, in 1970 the number of foreign-born residents in the U.S. was the lowest in a century. The share of the population that's foreign born today is about the same as the late 1800s and early 1900s, according to the U.S. Census.

Now What?

It is important to note that Trump's plan would have a steep uphill battle to get through this Congress. Still, not surprisingly, there is also debate around how Trump's drastic proposal will affect blue-collar wages moving forward. The Trump administration hopes the plan will free up future jobs for American low-wage workers. But Mark Zandi, Moody's chief economist, who has advised John McCain and donated to McCain and Hillary Clinton's campaigns, told Politico the plan is a "mistake" that will cause the labor force to come to a "standstill" in the next decade. "It is hard to imagine a policy that would do more damage to long-term economic growth," he said.

As NPR's Brian Naylor noted, economists believe the country's low unemployment rate (4.4 percent) coupled with retiring baby boomers will result in a labor shortage in the coming years.

Additionally, an open letter signed by 1,470 economists argued that "the benefits that immigration brings to society far outweigh their costs, and smart immigration policy could better maximize the benefits of immigration while reducing the costs."

On the campaign trail, President Trump praised highly skilled workers, which his plan now prioritizes — but studies are also mixed on whether those workers positively impact wages or also depress the wages of American-born workers.

Illegal Immigrants Pose an Economic Dilemma for Social Service Providers

Alex Nowrasteh

Alex Nowrasteh is a writer and the director of immigration studies at the Cato Institute's Center for Global Liberty and Prosperity.

Last week during one of their debates, all Democratic primary candidates supported government health care for illegal immigrants. This type of position is extremely damaging politically and, if enacted, would unnecessarily burden taxpayers for likely zero improvements in health outcomes. I expect the eventual Democratic candidate for president to not support this type of proposal, but it should be nipped in the bud.

After the debate, Democratic candidate Julian Castro argued that extending government health care to illegal immigrants would not be a big deal. "[W]e already pay for the health care of undocumented immigrants," Castro said. "It's called the emergency room. People show up in the emergency room and they get care, as they should." It is true that some illegal immigrants use emergency room services thanks to the Emergency Medical Treatment and Labor Act and to Emergency Medicaid, but Castro leaned heavily into a stereotype often used by nativists. According to a paper published in the journal *Health Affairs*, illegal immigrants between the ages of 18-64 consumed about $1.1 billion in government healthcare benefits in 2006 – about 0.13 percent of the approximately $867 billion in government healthcare expenditures that year. That's a fraction of the cost that would be imposed on American taxpayers by extending nationalized health care to all illegal immigrants. So, with all due respect to Mr. Castro, we do not already pay for their health care just because some illegal immigrants visit emergency rooms at government expense.

"Illegal Immigrants – and Other Non-Citizens – Should Not Receive Government Healthcare," by Alex Nowrasteh, The Cato Institute, July 9, 2019. Reprinted by permission.

One of the reasons why immigrants individually consume so much less welfare than native-born Americans is that many of them do not have legal access to these benefits. Cato scholars have proposed making these welfare restrictions even stricter to deny benefits to all non-citizens and to not count work credit toward entitlements until immigrants are naturalized citizens – what the late Bill Niskanen called "build a wall around the welfare state, not around the country."

Many American voters are concerned about immigrant consumption of welfare benefits. In a 2017 poll, 28 percent of Americans agreed with the statement that "Immigration detracts from our character and weakens the United States because it *puts too many burdens on government services*, causes language barriers, and creates housing problems [emphasis added]." That level of concern exists under current laws that restrict non-citizen access to benefits and even chill eligible non-citizen participation. I'd expect that poll result to worsen if new immigrants, especially illegal immigrants, were put on government health care program.

Extending government health care to illegal immigrants and other new immigrants would probably not improve healthcare outcomes for immigrants. According to the wonderful *The Integration of Immigrants into American Society* report published by the National Academies of Sciences, immigrants already have better infant, child, and adult health outcomes than native-born Americans, while also having less access to welfare benefits like Medicaid. Immigrants also live about 3.4 years longer than native-born Americans do. Illegal Mexican immigrants had an average of 1.6 fewer physician visits per year compared to native-born Americans of Mexican descent. Other illegal Hispanic immigrants made an average of 2.1 fewer visits to doctors per year than their native-born counterparts. Illegal immigrants are about half as likely to have chronic healthcare problems than native-born Americans. Overall per capita health care spending was 55 percent lower for immigrants than for native-born Americans.

Immigrants also lower the cost of other portions of the health care system. In 2014, immigrants paid 12.6 percent of all premiums to private health insurers but accounted for only 9.1 percent of all insurer expenditures. Immigrants' annual premiums exceeded their health care expenditures by $1,123 per enrollee, for a total of $24.7 billion. That offset the deficit of $163 per native-born enrollee. The immigrant net-subsidy persisted even after ten years of residence in the United States.

From 2002-2009, immigrants subsidized Medicare as they made 14.7 percent of contributions but only consumed 7.9 percent of expenditures, for a $13.8 billion annual surplus. By comparison, native-born Americans consumed $30.9 billion more in Medicare than they contributed annually. Among Medicare enrollees, average expenditures were $1,465 lower for immigrants than for native-born Americans, for a difference of $3,923 to $5,388. From 2000 to 2011, illegal immigrants contributed $2.2 to $3.8 billion more than they withdrew annually in Medicare benefits (a total surplus of $35.1 billion). If illegal immigrants had neither contributed to nor withdrawn from the Medicare Trust Fund during those 11 years, it would become insolvent 1 year earlier than currently predicted — in 2029 instead of 2030.

American taxpayers should not have to pay for the health care costs of other Americans, let alone for non-citizens. For those reading this post who are very concerned about the well-being of immigrants, think of what would happen to public support for legal immigration if welfare benefits were extended in this way. Immigrants come here primarily for economic opportunity, not for government health insurance. They tend to be healthier than native-born Americans and lower the price of health care for others as a result — but the point would likely change if the laws were different. Let's not build public support for reducing legal immigration, or increase reluctance to expand it, by extending government health care, at enormous public cost, to people who don't need it.

Companies Take Advantage of the Financial Situation of Illegal Immigrants

Travis Putnam Hill

Travis Putnam Hill is an investigative reporting fellow at the Texas Tribune.

At an hour when many people are tucking themselves in for the night, the cleaning crew at an Austin-area Target store is just getting started. By the time it finishes in the early morning, workers will have cleaned the bathrooms, taken out the garbage, washed windows and carpets and polished the floors to that reflective white sheen on which the Target Corporation prides itself.

One of those janitors — a 57-year-old Mexican immigrant who preferred to go by his nickname, "Chunco" — has worked for various contractors cleaning Target stores in Central Texas for about 12 years, despite lacking the legal right to work in the United States.

And he's not alone: "All of the [cleaning] workers I've known were undocumented," Chunco told The Texas Tribune, speaking in his native Spanish.

While his immigration status hasn't posed a significant roadblock to his continued employment, it has exposed him to the risks that come with working in the shadows. He and his fellow custodians have repeatedly been paid less than minimum wage and worked six or seven days a week with no overtime pay, according to court records and Texas Tribune interviews. In some cases, they accumulated those overtime hours when Target managers would lock them in the store for extra tasks.

"We've realized that [employers] prefer us for being undocumented because we just keep our heads down to get jobs,"

"Big employers no strangers to benefits of cheap, illegal labor," by Travis Putnam Hill, The Texas Tribune, December 19, 2016. Reprinted by permission.

Chunco said. "[We] can't afford to complain. They take advantage of us being undocumented."

What Chunco describes is a window into an expansive underground labor market in which illegal hiring is widespread, even among some of the biggest names in American business. Yet the risk of running afoul of immigration authorities is low. Employers skirt culpability by accepting fake documents that they are not legally required to verify, misclassifying workers as independent contractors or subcontracting to separate businesses that do the actual hiring — all while claiming they did what the law requires to verify their workers' employment authorization.

It's that "don't ask, don't tell" system that allows employers to benefit from cheap immigrant labor. The same shadows under which undocumented immigrants are hired can also obscure the further exploitation they often endure.

"The fact that they're in the shadows makes them vulnerable," said Bill Beardall, executive director of the Equal Justice Center, a nonprofit law firm that represents low-wage workers in Texas.

And he would know: A large portion of the center's cases involve unpaid and underpaid wages to immigrant workers. Two of its cases illustrate the nature of this abuse, and how brand-name employers attempt to distance themselves from such transgressions.

Locked In Without Pay

Back in 2007 to 2008, the Equal Justice Center represented Chunco and 28 other janitorial workers in a lawsuit against Target and a contractor called Jim's Maintenance for unpaid wages and overtime. According to publicly available court documents, Target's lawyers asserted that the retailer was not a joint employer of the workers and thus not responsible for the wages that Jim's Maintenance had failed to pay. Target instead claimed that the workers were employees solely of Jim's Maintenance.

To Beardall, the notion that these janitors were not jointly employed by Target was "preposterous."

"It was the Target night managers," he said, "who let [the workers] in the building and locked them [in], and told them what to do at night, and wouldn't let them out in the morning until the Target manager had walked around the store with the crew and said, 'I'll let you out.'"

The list of undisputed facts culled from hours of deposition testimony from parties on both sides of the suit reveals the degree of control Target had over the janitors. Target managers decided when shifts would start and directly told the workers when they should come in, which was usually around 10 or 11 p.m. Shifts were typically scheduled to end at 7 or 8 a.m., but Target managers regularly held the workers past the scheduled quitting time. And to ensure Target's strict cleaning standards were met, managers would frequently lock the workers in the store for the entirety of their shifts.

Depositions from both sides also showed that the janitors often worked 60 or more hours each week, yet according to testimony, were never paid overtime. While Target kept records of the workers' hours, Jim's Maintenance did no such thing and instead tracked only days worked. The wages the workers did receive often came out well below minimum wage — in at least one case to the equivalent of $4.35 an hour.

In 2006, Target terminated its contract with Jim's after an audit by Price Waterhouse Coopers found that Jim's had improperly misclassified multiple workers as independent contractors and failed to keep required wage and hour records. Testimony from a Target official revealed that, even after receiving audit findings, Target did not take steps to report the violations to the proper authorities. Instead, it cut ties with Jim's, giving the cleaning contractor just two days' notice.

The end of the contract put Jim's out of business since, as Beardall put it, "Its only function in life was to clean stores for Target." To make matters worse, Target decided to hold on to $496,000 in fees owed to Jim's for its services for the entire month of May 2006. As a result, Jim's couldn't afford to give the workers their final paycheck.

For its part, Jim's Maintenance acknowledged in briefs to the court that it did not pay workers the required overtime wages. The contractor contended, however, that it was merely a "labor recruiter" and "paymaster" rather than a joint employer and that Target was solely liable for the unpaid overtime, as it was the retailer who forced the workers to work long hours. The court ultimately rejected that argument, saying Jim's was, in fact, an employer.

The suit was eventually settled out of court, and Target never admitted any wrongdoing. An attorney who represented Jim's in the case did not respond to requests for comment.

In an emailed response, a Target spokeswoman wrote that the lawsuit "dealt exclusively with wage and hour issues" and did not raise questions about the plaintiffs' immigration status or that of anyone associated with Jim's Maintenance.

"We can find no references in the court record that would indicate that Target knew that plaintiffs, nor any other people, were 'undocumented,'" she wrote. "The issue instead was that their employer, Jim's Maintenance, was failing to fulfill its obligations to keep proper records, including records of I-9 compliance. This failure to fulfill its contractual obligations ultimately contributed to Target's decision to terminate its contract with Jim's Maintenance."

Court documents and a hearing transcript suggest the retailer's lawyers may have suspected the workers were undocumented and intended to use their legal status against them in the suit.

Target's lawyers sought to grill the workers in their depositions on matters related to their immigration status, specifically about the names and Social Security numbers the workers provided on their employment applications. They argued that if the workers had provided false information on their applications, it would speak to the credibility of their wage and hour complaints. But the Equal Justice Center filed a protective order to prohibit such questions, claiming it would have a "chilling effect" on the workers' ability to enforce their legitimate wage rights. The judge agreed that the workers suing Target did not have to answer questions related to their immigration status.

"Employment rights apply equally to all workers, regardless of their immigration status," Beardall said. "The problem is most undocumented workers don't know that, and employers may not know that. If they do know that, they will nevertheless use those workers' vulnerable immigration status to discourage them from enforcing their rights."

Case of the Fruit Cutters

A similar case unfolded between 2012 and 2013 when workers who cut, bagged and stocked fruit at H-E-B grocery stores filed a class action lawsuit claiming that they had been cheated out of minimum wage and overtime pay.

The workers — mostly immigrants and women — worked at H-E-B through a contractor called Pastrana's Produce, a company with offices in Brownsville and the Mexican border city of Matamoros. The lawsuit named both Pastrana's and H-E-B as defendants, but the Texas grocer denied responsibility.

"They were trying to contend that women who were cutting up fruit and nopal in their store to be sold in the produce rack and paid for at the checkout counter, that those women were contractors not of H-E-B but of something called Pastrana's Produce," Beardall said.

In sworn affidavits, the produce workers claimed they routinely worked seven days a week, often for 50 hours or more, but weren't compensated for overtime and did not receive an hourly wage. Instead, they were paid a set rate for each bag of produce that customers bought. That rate depended on the type of produce sold and tended to be so low that their paychecks never amounted to minimum wage.

One of the plaintiffs alleged that a manager at the H-E-B store on William Cannon Drive in Austin made her work in the cooler without any protective clothing — an allegation repeated by several others at different H-E-B locations.

To further exacerbate the problems, it seems the workers were discouraged from trying to recover their wages. According to the affidavits, some of the workers knew about a previous lawsuit between Pastrana's fruit cutters and H-E-B but didn't join at that time for fear of losing their jobs. They said a Pastrana's supervisor told them the workers who did join would lose the suit as well as their jobs.

As in the Target case, lawyers from the Equal Justice Center argued that the workers were jointly employed by H-E-B and Pastrana's because they were a vital part of H-E-B's business. They worked only in stores owned by H-E-B and under supervision of H-E-B managers, who determined their work hours and daily production.

And also like the Target case, the dispute was settled out of court, with H-E-B maintaining that it was not a joint employer.

By the time of publication, H-E-B had not responded to questions regarding the case. And attorneys for both sides remained tight-lipped both about the terms of the settlement and the specifics of the workers' immigration status — that is, whether they were authorized to work in the United States.

Michael Latimer, the lawyer who represented Pastrana's, said the plaintiffs' immigration status was never a question throughout the suit.

A woman who answered the door at the former addresses of one of the plaintiffs said she was a friend of the plaintiff and recalled him talking about his case against H-E-B. She also said he was undocumented.

The Texas Tribune was able to reach another plaintiff by phone, but when asked to verify whether the produce workers were undocumented, she hung up abruptly.

Elephant In the Room

The cases are just two examples of how average citizens reap the fruits of unauthorized labor on a daily basis, even if they may not realize it. Undocumented workers toil away on towering construction projects and harvest crops in sunbaked fields. They prepare food behind kitchen doors and wash the dishes when the meal is done. They build homes, mow lawns and clean stores and office buildings.

While many decry the scourge of undocumented immigrants taking jobs from Americans, they rarely address their anger at the businesses that hire those immigrants, businesses whose low prices may depend on the low wages they pay.

"What you end up with when you have a group of workers who are relegated to a second-class status is it stimulates a race to the bottom where some employers, the unscrupulous employers, prefer to hire those workers precisely because they're exploitable," Beardall said.

And so often, those exploitable workers are undocumented immigrants.

"It's the elephant in the room that nobody wants to talk about," Beardall said, speaking generally. "We live in a society where we don't really want to acknowledge that ... precisely because business depends on those workers."

Chunco's experience may attest to that dependence. For more than a decade, he has been on the payroll of a string of different companies contracted by Target to clean its stores.

"If a company doesn't meet the requirements that Target demands, [Target] breaks ties [with that company] and another one comes in," he said. "The next company comes in and asks Target if the workers are doing a good job. And if they say we're doing an excellent job, we keep our jobs with the new company."

So despite the lawsuit and dissolution of Jim's Maintenance, Chunco is still buffing the same Target floors in the same Target buildings that he has for the last 12 years. And the disadvantages of working in the shadows haven't quite disappeared: He said his schedule was cut to five hours per shift, but he's still required to do all the work he used to do in eight or 10.

"When you've been here for a while, you learn that they do exploit you," he said. "But we have to work."

CHAPTER 2

Do Sanctuary Cities Pose a Threat to Security and Well-Being?

A History of Sanctuary Cities in the United States

Robert Longley

Robert Longley is a writer and an urban planning expert. He has worked with several government agencies, including the Environmental Protective Agency and the US Census Bureau.

While the term has no specific legal definition, a "sanctuary city" in the United States is a city or county in which undocumented immigrants are protected from deportation or prosecution for violations of U.S. federal immigration laws.

In both a legal and practical sense, "sanctuary city" is a rather vague and informal term. It can, for example, indicate that the city has actually enacted laws that restrict what their police and other employees are allowed to do during encounters with undocumented immigrants. On the other hand, the term has also been applied to cities like Houston, Texas, which calls itself a "welcoming city" to undocumented immigrants but have no specific laws regarding enforcement of federal immigration laws.

In an example of a states' rights conflict arising from the U.S. system of federalism, sanctuary cities refuse to use any local funds or police resources to enforce the national government's immigration laws. Police or other municipal employees in sanctuary cities are not allowed to ask a person about their immigration, naturalization, or citizenship status for any reason. In addition, sanctuary city policies forbid police and other city employees from notifying federal immigration enforcement officers of the presence of undocumented immigrants living in or passing through the community.

Due to its limited resources and the scope of the immigration enforcement job, the U.S. Immigration and Customs Enforcement

"A Brief Overview of Sanctuary Cities," by Robert Longley, ThoughtCo, March 12, 2018. ThoughtCo is part of the Dotdash Publishing Family. Reprinted by permission.

Agency (ICE) must rely on local police to help enforce federal immigration laws. However, federal law does not require local police to locate and detain undocumented immigrants just because ICE requests they do so.

Sanctuary city policies and practices may be established by local laws, ordinances or resolutions, or simply by practice or custom.

In September 2015, the U.S. Immigration and Customs Enforcement Agency estimated that about 300 jurisdictions—cities and counties—nationwide had sanctuary city laws or practices. Examples of large U.S. cities with sanctuary laws or practices include San Francisco, New York City, Los Angeles, San Diego, Chicago, Houston, Dallas, Boston, Detroit, Seattle, and Miami.

U.S. "sanctuary cities" should not be confused with "cities of sanctuary" in the United Kingdom and Ireland that apply local policies of welcoming and encouraging the presence of refugees, asylum seekers, and others seeking safety from political or religious persecution in their countries of origin.

Brief History of Sanctuary Cities

The concept of sanctuary cities is far from new. The Old Testament's Book of Numbers speaks of six cities in which persons who had committed murder or manslaughter were allowed to claim asylum. From 600 CE until 1621 CE, all churches in England were allowed to grant sanctuary to criminals and some cities were designated as criminal and political sanctuaries by Royal charter.

In the United States, cities and counties began adopting immigrant sanctuary policies in the late 1970s. In 1979, the Los Angeles police department adopted an internal policy known as "Special Order 40," which stated, "Officers shall not initiate police action with the objective of discovering the alien status of a person. Officers shall not arrest nor book persons for violation of title 8, section 1325 of the United States Immigration code (Illegal Entry)."

Political and Legislative Actions on Sanctuary Cities

As the number of sanctuary cities grew over the next two decades, both the federal and state governments began taking legislative actions to require full enforcement of federal immigration laws.

On September 30, 1996, President Bill Clinton signed the Illegal Immigration Reform and Immigrant Responsibility Act of 1996 addressing the relationship between the federal government and local governments. The law focuses on illegal immigration reform and includes some of the toughest measures ever taken against illegal immigration. Aspects considered in the law include border enforcement, penalties for alien smuggling and document fraud, deportation and exclusion proceedings, employer sanctions, welfare provisions, and changes to existing refugee and asylum procedures. In addition, the law prohibits cities from banning municipal workers for reporting persons' immigration status to federal authorities.

A section of the Illegal Immigration Reform and Immigrant Responsibility Act of 1996 allows local police agencies to obtain training in the enforcement of federal immigration laws. However, it fails to provide state and local law enforcement agencies with any general powers for immigration enforcement.

Some States Oppose Sanctuary Cities

Even in some states housing sanctuary or sanctuary-like cities and counties, legislatures and governors have taken steps to ban them. In May 2009, Georgia's Governor Sonny Perdue signed state Senate Bill 269, a law prohibiting Georgia cities and counties from adopting sanctuary city policies.

In June 2009, Tennessee's Governor Phil Bredesen signed state Senate Bill 1310 banning local governments from enacting sanctuary city ordinances or policies.

In June 2011, Texas Governor Rick Perry called a special session of the state legislature to consider state Senate Bill 9, a proposed law banning sanctuary cities. While public hearings on the bill were held before the Texas Senate's Transportation and

Homeland Security Committee, it was never considered by the full Texas legislature.

In January 2017, Texas Governor Greg Abbott threatened to oust any local officials who promoted sanctuary city laws or policies. "We are working on laws that will ... ban sanctuary cities [and] remove from office any officer-holder who promotes sanctuary cities," stated Gov. Abbott.

President Trump Takes Action

On January 25, 2017 U.S. President Donald Trump signed an executive order titled "Enhancing Public Safety in the Interior of the United States," which, in part, directed the Secretary of Homeland Security and Attorney General to withhold funding in the form of federal grants from sanctuary jurisdictions that refuse to comply with federal immigration law.

Specifically, Section 8 (a) of the executive order states, "In furtherance of this policy, the Attorney General and the Secretary, in their discretion and to the extent consistent with law, shall ensure that jurisdictions that willfully refuse to comply with 8 U.S.C. 1373 (sanctuary jurisdictions) are not eligible to receive Federal grants, except as deemed necessary for law enforcement purposes by the Attorney General or the Secretary."

In addition, the order directed the Department of Homeland Security to begin issuing weekly public reports that include "a comprehensive list of criminal actions committed by aliens and any jurisdiction that ignored or otherwise failed to honor any detainers with respect to such aliens."

Sanctuary Jurisdictions Dig In

Sanctuary jurisdictions wasted no time in reacting to President Trump's action.

In his State of the State address, California's Governor Jerry Brown vowed to defy President Trump's action. "I recognize that under the Constitution, federal law is supreme and that Washington determines immigration policy," stated Gov. Brown. "But as a state, we can and have had a role to play … And let me be clear: we will defend everybody—every man, woman, and child—who has come here for a better life and has contributed to the well-being of our state."

Chicago Mayor Rahm Emanuel has pledged $1 million in city funds to create a legal defense fund for immigrants threatened with prosecution due to President Trump's order. "Chicago has in the past been a sanctuary city. … It always will be a sanctuary city," said the mayor.

On January 27, 2017, Salt Lake City Mayor Ben McAdams stated he would refuse to enforce President Trump's order. "There has been fear and uncertainty among our refugee population the last few days," McAdams said. "We want to reassure them that we love them and their presence is an important part of our identity. Their presence makes us better, stronger and richer."

In Tragic 2015 Shooting, Sanctuary Cities Stir Debate

The tragic July 1, 2015 shooting death of Kate Steinle thrust sanctuary city laws into the center of controversy.

While visiting San Francisco's Pier 14, the 32-year old Steinle was killed by a single bullet fired from a pistol admittedly held at the time by Jose Ines Garcia Zarate, an undocumented immigrant.

Garcia Zarate, a citizen of Mexico, had been deported several times and had been convicted for illegal re-entry into the United States. Days before the shooting, he had been released from a San Francisco jail after a minor drug charge against him was dismissed. Although U.S. immigration officials had issued an order that police detain him, Garcia Zarate was released under San Francisco's sanctuary city laws.

The uproar over sanctuary cities grew on December 1, 2017, when a jury acquitted Garcia Zarate of charges of first-degree murder, second-degree murder, manslaughter, finding him guilty only of illegally possessing a fire arm.

In his trial, Garcia Zarate claimed he had just found the gun and that the shooting of Steinle had been an accident.

In acquitting him, the jury found reasonable doubt in Garcia Zarate's accidental shooting claim, and under the Constitution's guarantee of "due process of law," guarantee, his criminal record, history of prior convictions, and immigration status were not allowed to be presented as evidence against him.

Critics of permissive immigration laws reacted to the case by complaining that sanctuary city laws too often allow dangerous, criminal illegal immigrants to remain on the streets.

The Nullification Crisis and Its Relevance for Today's Sanctuary Cities

Hans A. von Spakovsky

Hans A. von Spakovsky is a former member of the Federal Election Committee and an attorney. He is now a writer and manager at the Heritage Foundation.

Y ou may not have heard of the "Nullification Crisis" that President Andrew Jackson faced in 1832. But there are many unfortunate similarities between it and what is happening today on immigration. From the unjustified obstruction of immigration law by some activist federal judges to the defiance of the federal government on sanctuary policies by governors and city mayors such as Ed Murray of Seattle, there are some interesting parallels — and lessons.

I was reminded of the Nullification Crisis recently on a tour of James Madison's home, Montpelier, which is close to the University of Virginia in Charlottesville, Virginia. One of the docents related how President Jackson had visited Madison in the midst of his reelection campaign to get his advice. This crisis was about high tariffs which, before the implementation of the income tax in 1913 through the Sixteenth Amendment, was one of the main sources of income for the federal government.

High tariff rates were resented throughout the South, particularly in South Carolina. While they benefited manufacturers in the northern states, they hurt the mostly agricultural southern states. Led by John Calhoun, South Carolina and other states asserted that they had the final authority to declare federal laws unconstitutional and thus null and void within their states. While Jackson was a moderate on tariffs and respectful of the rights states retained in our federal system, he was scornful of the nullification

"Sanctuary Cities? That's a Constitutional 'Hell No,'" by Hans A. von Spakovsky, The Heritage Foundation, April 18, 2017. Reprinted by permission.

theory. He considered it an unconstitutional, "abominable doctrine" that "will dissolve the Union."

In 1832, the nullifiers took control of the South Carolina government and passed the infamous "Ordinance of Nullification." They expressed the same type of virulent hostility and contempt for (and defiance of) the Jackson administration and the tariff system that we are seeing today towards the Trump administration over enforcement of federal immigration law, including provisions against certain sanctuary policies. Those states and cities are pushing the same concept of nullification of federal law, although they are doing it in federal court.

As one would expect of Andrew Jackson, he reacted strongly to this threat from South Carolina, including issuing a Nullification Proclamation on Dec. 10, 1832. Nullification was "incompatible with the existence of the Union, contradicted expressly by the letter of the Constitution, unauthorized by its spirit, inconsistent with every principle on which it was founded, and destructive of the great object for which it was formed," he wrote. The crisis was resolved by a compromise bill on tariffs that Congress passed in 1833 after passing the Force Bill, which gave the president the power to use state militias and federal forces against the nullifiers.

The similarity between these events and what is happening today are eerie. While there are many areas over which the states and the federal government share responsibility — or where the Tenth Amendment gives responsibility to the states — immigration is not one of them. Section 8 of Article I gives Congress exclusive authority to "establish a uniform Rule of Naturalization," just as Section 8 gives Congress the exclusive authority to establish and collect all "Imposts and Excises" or tariffs. The states have no authority in these areas at all. They can no more dispute the immigration rules established by Congress than they could dispute the tariffs imposed by Congress back in 1832.

This makes perfect sense. Any other rule would produce chaos. Think of the enormous problems that would be caused by border states such as Texas or California deciding that they would ignore federal law and apply their own immigration rules to individuals coming across the Mexican border into the United States — or if states decided that they would impose their own tariffs on foreign goods coming into their states in addition to those imposed by the federal government. In fact, it was that kind of behavior that was restricting trade under the Articles of Confederation between states such as Virginia and Maryland that helped lead to the call for a constitutional convention.

When it comes to immigration and the entry of aliens into the U.S., Congress delegated to the president the extremely broad authority under 8 U.S.C. §1182 (f) to suspend the entry of any aliens or class of aliens into the U.S. if he believes it "would be detrimental to the interests of the United States." As five dissenting judges at the Ninth Circuit Court of Appeals recently pointed out, there are a long series of decisions by the U.S. Supreme Court upholding the authority of prior presidents under this provision and severely limiting the ability of the courts to review the president's decision.

Unfortunately, at the urging of certain states, the courts have in large part ignored the Constitution, federal law, and prior precedents. They are instead substituting their judgment for that of the president, and enjoining the president's executive order by implementing a temporary halt to entry from certain terrorist safe havens. In essence, states such as Hawaii and Washington are turning to activist federal judges to nullify the exclusive authority of the federal government over immigration and the security of our national border — and those judges are complying.

The sanctuary policies implemented by cities such as San Francisco and Seattle also seek to nullify federal immigration law and obstruct its enforcement. 8 U.S.C. §1373 prohibits states and local jurisdictions from preventing their law enforcement officials from exchanging information with federal officials on the citizenship status of individuals they have arrested or detained. The Supreme Court upheld this provision in 2012 in *Arizona v. United States*.

Quite appropriately, Attorney General Jeff Sessions has announced that he will not award any discretionary federal grants from the Justice Department to cities that violate §1373. Seattle has filed suit, claiming that the federal government has no right to cut off its access to discretionary funding. The city also makes the meritless claims that its policy does not violate federal immigration law.

Sanctuary cities are claiming that Sessions is trying to force them to enforce federal immigration law and that the loss of federal funds would violate the holding in *NFIB v. Sebelius* (2012). This is the Supreme Court decision that upheld Obamacare but found that the Medicaid portion of Obamacare, which required states to significantly expand their Medicaid coverage or risk losing *all* Medicaid funding, violated the Spending Clause of the Constitution. The federal government was "commandeering" the states by compelling them to "enact or administer a federal regulatory program."

But Sessions is simply trying to get states to not obstruct federal enforcement. That includes abiding by the ban contained in Section 1373. Sanctuary cities are trying to prevent federal officials from finding out about criminal alien murderers, rapists, and other violent criminals that these cities would apparently rather release than have picked up and deported so they cannot further victimize Americans. Section 1373 doesn't force local law enforcement officials to notify federal officials when they detain an illegal alien; It simply says that local governments can't *ban* law enforcement officials from doing so.

The spurious legal argument that §1373 violates the anti-commandeering principle was raised by the City of New York in a lawsuit against the federal government only 11 days after the provision became federal law. New York also had a policy in place that forbade city officials from transmitting information on the immigration status of any individual to federal immigration authorities. In *City of New York v. U.S.* (1999), the Second Circuit Court of Appeals threw out the city's case because the federal law was constitutional and well within congressional authority on immigration.

As the court pointed out, §1373 does not compel "state and local governments to enact or administer any federal regulatory program. Nor has it affirmatively conscripted states, localities, or their employees into the federal government's service." The only thing the provision does is prohibit state and local governmental entities or officials from "directly restricting the voluntary exchange of immigration information with the INS." A contrary holding would cause chaos: "If Congress may not forbid states from outlawing even voluntary cooperation with federal programs by state and local officials, states will at times have the power to frustrate effectuation of some programs."

That is clearly what is happening here: sanctuary states and cities want to "frustrate effectuation" of federal enforcement of our immigration laws. The absence of such cooperation, as the Second Circuit said, would force federal officials to "resort to legal processes in every routine or trivial matter, often a practical impossibility." This was the same type of resistance exhibited by local governments to *Brown v. Board of Education*: "a refusal by local government to cooperate until under a court order to do so."

Furthermore, refusing to award sanctuary cities funds that have to be applied for and that are entirely discretionary within the judgement of the attorney general does not come anywhere close to "commandeering" a "State's legislative or administrative apparatus for federal purposes," which was the key factor in the NFIB decision. The Supreme Court said that there is no violation of the Spending Clause "when a State has a legitimate choice whether to accept the federal conditions in exchange for federal funds."

States can make their own decisions on whether to apply for a portion of the $4.1 billion the Justice Department has available to local jurisdictions for improving their law enforcement programs. In fact, this situation raises even fewer concerns than a federal law that the Supreme Court upheld in *South Dakota v. Dole* (1987). That law provided that states would lose five percent of their federal highway funds if they did not raise the drinking age to 21. This was "relatively mild encouragement" compared to the Medicaid expansion in Obamacare, where the Court described the potential loss of all Medicaid funding as a "gun to the head."

Similarly, when it comes to sanctuary cities, the Justice Department isn't threatening the cutoff of any major entitlement funds such as Medicaid or even state highway funds. What's at stake are discretionary grants that the states may or may not decide to apply for, and which the Justice Department may or may not choose to grant.

The Nullification Crisis was resolved when South Carolina rescinded its nullification ordinance after President Jackson issued his Nullification Proclamation. We can only hope that the current nullification crisis will also be resolved once and for all when all of the lawsuits being filed by the states to prevent the enforcement of federal immigration law reach the Supreme Court.

President Trump's Threat to Remove Funding from Sanctuary Cities Makes Them More Dangerous

Oliver Laughland, Julia Carrie Wong, and Sabrina Siddiqui

Oliver Laughland, Julia Carrie Wong, and Sabrina Siddiqui are all reporters for the Guardian US.

An executive order on "sanctuary cities" signed by Donald Trump on Wednesday has placed in the crosshairs over 400 cities and counties that offer some form of safe haven to America's 11 million undocumented migrants.

These localities include some of the largest, most progressive metropolises in the United States, many of which have already begun preparations to fight one of Trump's most aggressive campaign pledges—to force compliance with federal immigration agencies in a bid to ramp up deportations. The beginnings of that pledge have now been formalised by executive action within Trump's first week in office.

The order issued on Wednesday claims these jurisdictions "willfully violate federal law" causing "immeasurable harm to the American people," and instructs the Department of Homeland Security (DHS) and the US Department of Justice (DoJ) to explore which cities could be in violation of federal law and ways of stripping sanctuary jurisdictions of federal grant money, which amounts to billions of dollars across many different federal departments.

The order also instructs the US attorney general to explore "appropriate enforcement action" against any local government agency it deems to be in violation of a broad federal law that encourages—but does not compel—communication between local authorities and the DHS.

Trump's mandate also issues an extraordinary instruction to the DHS to publish a weekly list of so-called "criminal actions" committed by undocumented migrants and publicly announce which jurisdictions had previously "ignored or otherwise failed" to detain the accused individuals.

Researchers at the American Immigration Council concluded in a 2015 report that undocumented immigrants "are less likely to commit serious crimes or be behind bars than the native-born, and high rates of immigration are associated with lower rates of violent crime and property crime."

Although they vary by jurisdiction, sanctuary laws often prevent local law enforcement from aiding federal immigration authorities to identify undocumented migrants who are eligible for deportation unless they have been charged with severe crimes. Supporters argue these policies encourage cooperation and trust between large undocumented communities and local police. Critics argue, with little statistical evidence, that the policies result in dangerous criminal migrants being allowed to remain in the US.

Trump's order is broad, and will require substantial review by the DHS and DoJ and potentially legislative reform in Congress, but it is an aggressive statement of intent that has already provoked anger from powerful local politicians.

The New York attorney general, Eric Schneiderman, said on Wednesday that Trump "lacks the constitutional authority to cut off funding to states and cities simply because they have lawfully acted to protect immigrant families.

"Local governments seeking to protect their immigrant communities from federal overreach have every right to do so," Schneiderman said in a statement.

"Any attempt to bully local governments into abandoning policies that have proven to keep our cities safe is not only unconstitutional, but threatens the safety of our citizens."

He added: "I urge President Trump to revoke this executive order right away. If he does not, I will do everything in my power to fight it."

New York's mayor, Bill De Blasio, who has vowed to preserve sanctuary laws in the city, said on Wednesday that Trump's order carried grave security threats for the city as federal anti-terror funding could be at stake.

"President Trump issued an executive order today and its reported purpose was to enhance public safety, but here in New York City and in cities across nation, this executive order could in fact undermine public safety and make it left safe," De Blasio said.

"It could undermine relationships between police and communities … and second, potential funding cuts would come first and foremost from the NYPD," said De Blasio.

Federal money at risk included $156m in urban area security funding, $110m of which goes towards anti-terrorism efforts, De Blasio said.

The mayor on Tuesday announced an $84.7bn budget that skirted assumptions about any federal cutbacks from the Trump administration. Nonetheless, some city politicians said on Wednesday the signal of intent from the new president could "wipe out every dollar" of city savings.

Chicago's mayor, Rahm Emanuel, a former chief of staff to Barack Obama, has also vowed to preserve his city's sanctuary status.

The sentiment of uneasy resilience was echoed on the west coast by the Los Angeles mayor, Eric Garcetti, who argued Trump's order would result in severe economic and public safety repercussions.

"Splitting up families and cutting funding to any city—especially Los Angeles, where 40% of the nation's goods enter the US at our port, and more than 80m passengers traveled through our airport last year—puts the personal safety and economic health of our entire nation at risk. It is not the way forward for the United States," Garcetti said in a statement.

Both Garcetti and Ed Lee, the mayor of San Francisco, another major sanctuary city, have announced additional legal services for immigrants since Trump's election, citing their commitment to protecting undocumented residents.

The San Francisco city attorney is also exploring whether it could pursue legal action against the federal government if it withholds funds, according to the San Francisco Chronicle.

Federal grant money is usually administered through two different mechanisms, either through discretionary funding that is awarded to local authorities or non-government entities following a competitive application process, or formula funding that is mandatorily administered through legislation.

In theory, the latter of these two mechanisms would be harder for the Trump administration to revoke. But a source with knowledge of the administration's thinking on the matter said the White House could argue that these formula grants could be revoked by arguing that the local authority being targeted had broken the law and was therefore in violation of terms of the grant.

Trump's efforts will also face a serious fightback from Democrats in Congress.

Nancy Pelosi, the House minority leader, accused Trump of "turning his back on both our history and our values as a proud nation of immigrants."

Pelosi's district falls entirely within San Francisco, where the 2015 murder of Kathryn Steinle, allegedly by a man who was in the country illegally, was seized on by Trump and conservatives to hit back against sanctuary cities. The suspect, Francisco Lopez-Sanchez, had previously been turned over to authorities in San Francisco by the federal Bureau of Prisons—but a lapse in communication over an arrest warrant prompted him to be released before Steinle's murder.

"Law-abiding, hard-working immigrant families deserve better than the Trump administration's radical xenophobia," Pelosi said in a statement.

The Congressional Hispanic Caucus (CHC), slammed the president for what they dubbed "draconian" actions.

"These executive orders fail to provide any practical solution to our nation's broken immigration system," New Mexico representative Michelle Lujan Grisham, the chairwoman of the CHC, told reporters on a conference call on Tuesday.

The efforts, she added, "are aimed at tearing apart families and breaking any hope of productive economic reform."

Sanctuary Cities Stand in the Way of Effective Policing

Jeff Proctor

Jeff Proctor is a writer at the Santa Fe Reporter *who has written about the New Mexico criminal justice system since 2002.*

The Santa Fe Police Department generally prefers to make its own law enforcement decisions. On paper, that means leaving federal immigration authorities in the dark on cases involving people who may be in the country illegally, even as President Donald Trump threatens cities' funding if they don't cooperate in fulfilling his campaign promise to cleanse the nation of "criminal illegal aliens."

But during the past two-plus years, SFPD has tipped off Immigration and Customs Enforcement (ICE) at least three times about suspected undocumented immigrants. Details about the cases highlight difficulties in balancing public safety against remaining true to "sanctuary" policies that, in Santa Fe, were born of cooperation and core values but are now bound to experience some turbulence.

For Ronald Ayala-Santos, according to police, a heads-up for the feds took some doing on his part.

Since mid-2015, the 20-year-old has admitted to making a false report about "heavily armed men" swarming a Santa Fe neighborhood and phoning in bogus bomb threats that led to the chaotic clearing of the Violet Crown Cinema and the Plaza, police say.

Ayala-Santos was indicted on several misdemeanors and a fourth-degree felony charge after police linked him to the Violet Crown incident, court records show. And after the alleged threat on the Plaza in September, he was arrested.

"Uneasy Sanctuary," by Jeff Proctor, Santa Fe Reporter, February 14, 2016. Reprinted by permission.

But it wasn't until he posted bond, was released from the Santa Fe County Adult Detention Center and created yet another bomb scare—this time at the Plaza Café Southside—that city police say they decided to tell ICE that Ayala-Santos may be in the country illegally.

"At some point, enough is enough," SFPD Sgt. Craig Ernst says in an interview, emphasizing what he calls Ayala-Santos' ongoing, escalating pattern of behavior and the mayhem his threats have caused. "The agency does have a responsibility to safeguard the community."

Ernst did not know whether ICE has pursued him, and the agency did not respond to requests for comment for this story.

On Jan. 31, prosecutors dropped the case stemming from the incident on the Plaza although the charges could be refiled later.

Ernst says detectives followed SFPD policy by running the decision to notify ICE about Ayala-Santos up the chain of command to a high-ranking officer. Still, the case represents a rare but not unheard of practice for a police department that reports to a mayor who has become a prominent figure in the national "sanctuary city" movement.

Mayor Javier Gonzales has yet to endorse either of two proposals that would tweak the city's sanctuary policies.

"The mayor would be in support of what passed last night, but he is also interested in seeing what Councilor Harris' amendments might be before making a final call," said city spokesman Matt Ross.

The city's finance committee on Monday passed a proposal, sponsored by councilors Joseph Maestas and Renee Villarreal, that prohibits city employees from disclosing identifying information of anyone who comes into contact with local authorities. Other provisions would improve language access services and develop policies for police to process special visas for crime victims.

Turnout was unusually high for a finance committee hearing, with nearly 200 locals packing council chambers to support the Maestas/Villarreal measure.

Business leaders, legal advocates and local officials, including former mayor David Coss, all spoke in support of the proposal. "I just ask that you work with us and collaborate to ensure all our children and family feel safe in our schools," said Veronica Garcia, superintendent of Santa Fe Public Schools.

Santa Feans came out in droves, despite recent changes to the resolution intended to put the city on better legal footing should President Trump make good on his threats to yank federal funding from sanctuary jurisdictions. Sponsors recently stripped the term "sanctuary" from earlier drafts.

Still, even popular ideas don't pass without controversy. City Councilor Michael Harris on Friday introduced an alternate sanctuary resolution that is significantly shorter than the proposal offered by Villarreal and Maestas. Harris' text does not include as many actionable provisions, but does list statistics showing that sanctuary communities have lower crime rates. Another line makes clear Santa Fe's "commitment to the established rule of law."

Meanwhile, Santa Fe County has never embraced the "sanctuary" label, though its policies and practices hew closely to jurisdictions that do, such as the city of Santa Fe. For example, the county jail does not honor so-called "ICE detainer requests," in which the federal agency asks city and county jailers to hold suspected undocumented immigrants beyond when they could otherwise have been released.

"The way I look at it, for liability and litigation purposes, I can only hold someone until a release order comes from a [state] judge," says Derek Williams, the jail's new warden. "It's a potential civil rights violation otherwise."

In 2012, the county drew a rebuke from ICE for its refusal to cooperate. ICE has backed off since then, according to data gathered by the Transactional Records Access Clearinghouse at Syracuse University in New York. In the federal fiscal year 2012, ICE requested 155 immigration detainers from the Santa Fe County jail. In fiscal 2015, that number had plummeted to just 12. Williams, who began his tenure a month ago, did not know how many of the requests had been granted.

Marcela Diaz of the immigrant rights group Somos Un Pueblo Unido says the communities she represents are not hung up on the "sanctuary" label. Strong policies that protect people regardless of immigration status matter more, she says, and both the city and county have those.

"And what matters more than that is openness and transparency: knowing that when officers or the jail make a mistake—and everyone does—people can trust that complaints are taken seriously and they have a safe place for the redress of grievances," Diaz tells SFR. "That's what 'sanctuary' really means."

For years, Somos Un Pueblo Unido and other immigrant groups have worked well with city and county officials, she says. But with a relatively new chief at SFPD (Patrick Gallagher took over the post permanently a year ago), a new warden at the jail and the Trump administration promising federal dollars for cooperation in enforcement, there is work to do to maintain the delicate balance in Santa Fe.

"We've had good experiences in the past, and I want to believe that these individuals want what our community wants: a sense of belonging and safety," Diaz says. "But when I read a quote from the new police chief saying, 'We're not going to turn anyone over to ICE unless they're a criminal,' well, he just said what Donald Trump said. And we all know that's bullsh*t."

Of course, entering the US without documentation is technically a crime in itself—one Diaz says city and county officials in Santa Fe have largely shielded immigrants from, regardless of status.

Learning about Ayala-Santos' case from SFR raised some concerns for Diaz, though she declined to comment in detail without reviewing the entire case file. So did the two other cases in which SFPD has, according to Deputy Chief Mario Salbidrez, cooperated with ICE during the past two-plus years: once after burglary suspect Carlos Navarrete-May told officers in December he was connected to a Mexican drug cartel, and another time when an SFPD officer saw Jorge Serrano-Nevarez at the burning of Zozobra in September 2015.

Serrano-Nevarez had been deported after serving federal prison time for property crimes, and the officer called ICE to obtain a warrant for illegal re-entry. The agency issued the warrant, and the officer later arrested him.

The department's policies prohibit officers from making arrests solely based on a person's immigration status—or from notifying ICE that a criminal suspect is in the country illegally, except in cases involving certain felonies, most of them violent crimes.

That doesn't mean ICE won't come looking on its own. In Santa Fe, the federal agency has taken away immigrant residents who lack legal documentation to live here. In recent weeks, the Trump administration has ramped up immigration enforcement in cities across the country, and an executive order signed during the new president's first week in office seeks to deputize local police and sheriffs to assist that effort while withholding federal funds from cities and counties that don't.

Diaz says Trump's carrot-and-stick approach may create difficult decisions for officials who have resisted aiding ICE, particularly in cash-strapped times like those New Mexico cities are facing.

Santa Fe County Commissioner Robert Anaya said he has never favored embracing the "sanctuary" label because it is a designation without a distinction. Further, he points out that the county's federal funding has come through rigorous request for proposals and grant writing processes.

"It would be ludicrous for the president or anyone else to come in and say you won't get this funding anymore when we complied with the terms of those processes," he said. "I would expect there would be all kinds of litigation if they tried to take those dollars back. There would be due process and other issues, but now that you mention it, I guess some of that may be out the window now."

Sanctuary Cities Are Constitutional by Definition

America's Voice Education Fund

America's Voice Education Fund is a media organization that seeks to tell stories about immigration to create public and policy-based change in the United States.

S anctuary cities" is actually a misnomer. While many Americans believe that it refers to a city that doesn't prosecute immigrants, so-called "sanctuary cities" actually refer to something far more specific.

There's no single definition of what is a sanctuary city, but generally speaking, it's a city (or a county, or a state) that limits its cooperation with federal immigration enforcement agents in order to protect low-priority immigrants from deportation, while still turning over those who have committed serious crimes. This is why we prefer the term "safe cities."

What Is a Sanctuary/Safe City?

Safe cities come into play when an undocumented immigrant comes into contact with the police. A very common occurrence of this happens on the road—someone is speeding, has a broken taillight, or has a broken license plate light, and is pulled over. If a person is undocumented, chances are they do not have a valid driver's license—only twelve states and the District of Columbia allow immigrants to legally drive. Immigrants still have to get to work and school somehow—but being found without a valid driver's license can get an individual arrested.

Other reasons immigrants (just like native-born Americans) come into contact with the police include an immigrant calling

"Immigration 101: What is a Sanctuary/Safe City?" America's Voice Education Fund, March 8, 2018. Reprinted by permission.

the police to their house (for example in the case of a domestic dispute), a car accident, drug usage, police checkpoints, so forth.

Once an immigrant is arrested, their information gets put into a federal database that is shared with Immigration and Customs Enforcement (ICE). ICE can then issue a hold, also called a detainer, asking the police to hold that person in custody until ICE can come pick that person up for immigration detention and eventual deportation.

Here's where we get to important legal point #1: being undocumented *is not a crime*. It's a civil violation. Undocumented immigrants have rights under the U.S. Constitution. And according to due process, the police cannot detain anyone who hasn't at least been suspected of a crime. If a police officer encounters someone walking down the street who turns out to be undocumented, they cannot arrest that person because that person has not committed a crime (ICE, however, can). Similarly, if the police arrest someone undocumented—for example, someone suspected of committing a crime, who is then cleared, they must let that person go.

Important legal point #2: holding an immigrant past the point when they should be released, just so that ICE can pick them up, is unconstitutional. Multiple courts have said so, and immigrants can sue the police for unlawful holding.

Here we get back to the point of safe cities: in a safe city, the police will release an arrested immigrant after he's been cleared of charges, posted bail, or completed jail time for whatever he was arrested for. A non-safe city will hold that person until ICE can come pick them up—*even though that extra holding is not constitutional.*

Keep in mind that all of the above only applies if the undocumented person has not committed any serious crimes. If they have, the police can keep them in jail by filing charges. Or ICE can present the police with a warrant or other order from a judge, which will result in a hold until ICE can come by.

The Case of Alex

Here's a pretty real-life example of how this works: let's take "Alex," someone who is in the US without papers (and who is not a Dreamer). One day, Alex gets pulled over the police because his taillight is broken. The police find out that he has no driver's license. They take Alex and put him in jail overnight because of the driver's license infraction; otherwise Alex has no criminal record whatsoever. While Alex is in jail, the police puts his information into the federal database shared with ICE, and ICE puts a hold / detainer on him.

Remember: Alex is in jail for a driver's license infraction. He has not committed any other crimes. The fact that he is an undocumented immigrant is not a crime. The police can hold him for what he's done—drive without a license. But holding him past the time when he should be released, just so that immigration agents can come pick him up, is unconstitutional.

If Alex doesn't live in a safe city, the police might hold him for days or longer until immigration agents pick him up, which might put Alex on the path to deportation even though he's done nothing besides drive without a license. Even though this is currently what many cities and counties do—even though this is what the Trump Administration wants cities and counties to do—it's illegal because it robs immigrants like Alex of due process.

If Alex does live in a safe city, the police would recognize that Alex has not committed any serious crimes and release him (in this example) after his one night in jail. That's what they're supposed to do. That's why some also suggest that we call safe cities "constitutional cities."

Why Are Safe Cities Important?

Safe Cities Are Safer

In a sentence, safe cities make everyone safer. This is because:

- The police can focus on going after serious criminals, rather than arresting or detaining immigrants just for being undocumented
- Cities, communities, and law enforcement *want* undocumented immigrants to trust the police. In order for the police to be most effective at their jobs, they need to be able to work with immigrants who report crimes, give tips, or testify as witnesses. In order for immigrants to trust the police, they need to know that an interaction with law enforcement won't lead to their deportation.

Research backs this up; one analysis has shown that safe cities see 15% less crime than non-safe cities. Another found that two-thirds of the cities that had the highest jumps in murder rates in 2016 were not safe cities—in fact, they are the opposite, generally eager to hold immigrants for ICE pick-up and detention.

In contrast, scary things can happen when immigrants become afraid of the police. In Houston, the police chief noted that the number of Hispanics reporting rape is down 42.8% from last year, and the number reporting other violent crimes has dropped 13%. This is during a year when crimes reported by non-Hispanics increased. Immigrants in California also aren't reporting sex crimes, while fears of deportation caused women in Colorado to drop domestic abuse cases in which they were witnesses.

Police Departments Support Safe City Policies

That's why so many law enforcement officers support safe city policies. That includes the Fraternal Order of Police, a membership organization which endorsed Donald Trump in the 2016 election but has since told him to back off the idea of punishing cities or their police departments for immigrant-friendly safe city policies.

What Does Trump Want with Safe Cities?

The Trump Administration, and especially Attorney General Jeff Sessions, has repeatedly tried to target safe cities. They get in the way of the Administration's mass deportation efforts, and Sessions has repeatedly threatened to defund them. But the law here is on the cities' side, partly due to a conservative pet cause: states' rights.

Safe Cities and States' Rights

It's ironic and hypocritical for Republican lawmakers to demand the safe cities and counties handle immigrants the way Trump and Sessions want cities and counties to handle them, because conservatives are supposed to support protecting local government from federal intrusion. Luckily, there are pretty solid Supreme Court rulings—some written by conservative justices—that protect states from the Trump Administration's demands over safe city policies. According to the courts:

- The federal government cannot place conditions on grants to states and localities unless the conditions are "unambiguously" stated in the law
- The federal government cannot "commandeer" state and local officials to help them enforce federal law (for example, the government forcing the police to hold immigrants for ICE agents)
- The federal government cannot coerce states or localities into action with a financial "gun to the head"

The History of the Trump Administration and Safe Cities

Even though the Trump Administration is wrong on safe cities, it has repeatedly tried to attack them—and immigrant communities. In March 2018, Sessions announced that he was filing a lawsuit against California and state policies which he deemed too immigrant friendly. Except, as Mark Joseph Stern at Slate wrote:

> Sessions didn't have the guts to go after California's principal sanctuary law because he would undoubtedly lose. Instead, he has targeted three secondary policies that make up a small portion of the state's broader immigration regime. Even if Sessions succeeded in overturning all three laws, California would remain a sanctuary state. But he probably won't succeed in

killing any of them. Perhaps this lawsuit is just another desperate attempt to win back President Donald Trump's affections.

Sessions is targeting 1) a rule that bars California law enforcement agencies from sharing information about undocumented immigrants, 2) a state law that protects immigrants from workplace raids, and 3) an act allowing the California attorney general to inspect immigration detention facilities within the state. Stern noted that all three components of Sessions' lawsuit effort are likely doomed, saying:

> Sessions, a self-proclaimed defender of states' rights, is seeking to undermine states' ability to conduct their own affairs. He is intruding upon California's police powers and undermining its protection of civil rights because he dislikes the state's laws. Sessions may wish that every state would accede to his policy agenda. But he can't use the Constitution to make them obey his commands.

Recently, the Department of Homeland Security and Acting ICE Director Thomas Homan have threatened local elected officials themselves for actions they've taken and actions their jurisdictions have taken to protect immigrants. As the ACLU wrote, these threats are "lawless and baseless." Moreover:

> The idea of these prosecutions is insidious. At bottom, the administration's complaint is that localities are adopting policies with which it disagrees. This idea of locking up elected officials for their political speech, beliefs, and votes is contrary to the First Amendment and the democratic principles on which our country was founded. Even the suggestion is dangerous and reprehensible.

Jeff Sessions' Department of Justice Letters
In April 2017, Sessions sent a letter to nine jurisdictions (one state, four cities, and four counties), telling them to get their safe city policies right with the Trump Administration, or else lose part of a $265 million grant intended to help police and prosecutors.

Except the threat in Sessions' letter was ignorant of how immigration law works. What Sessions' letter wanted the jurisdictions to do was obey a 1996 statute that says a city/county/state cannot prevent an official from talking to the feds about the immigration status of an individual. Almost every city and county in the country *is* in compliance with this requirement, including those that the Trump Administration considers to be safe cities. That part of the law is not even in dispute—yet Sessions for some reason saw fit to put jurisdictions on notice over it.

What Sessions (and Trump) ultimately want, of course, is for cities and counties to hold undocumented immigrants for ICE pickup and detention. But as explained above, when an immigrant has committed no crime, holding them for ICE is not consistent with current law, and cities and counties can be held liable for violating immigrants' rights. Sessions was unable to explain away this incoherence during a meeting with the mayors of the cities he targeted, and the mayors eventually left confused. On a number of immigration issues, "we hear very different messages from (Homeland Security), DOJ and also the White House," said Jorge Elorza, the Mayor of Providence, RI. "Just give us clarity and please have one, clear policy so we can know where we stand."

In addition, for all of about two weeks, the Trump Administration published a weekly report of cities and counties that operated safe city policies. Except, as explained above, cities that *don't* hold immigrants for ICE are operating in accordance with the law, while cities that *do* hold immigrants for ICE are behaving unconstitutionally—even though this is the opposite of what the Trump Administration wants to be true. A number of cities and counties clapped back against the Trump Administration for trying to name and shame them even though they were just following the law, forcing the Administration to apologize to a number of them and—after just a couple of weeks—stop publishing the reports altogether.

Trump's Executive Order Trying to Defund Safe Cities

In January 2017, Trump signed an executive order calling on safe cities to comply with federal immigration law or else have federal funding pulled. But in April, a San Francisco judge blocked the order, saying that the president had overstepped his powers by trying to tie billions in federal funding to immigration enforcement, and that only Congress could place such conditions on spending. The judge also noted that federal funding conditions must be tied to the policy in question—for example, housing funds cannot be conditional on immigration laws.

Just as the judge striking down Trump's Muslim ban did, the San Francisco judge used the words of the Trump Administration against itself, to prove that the intent behind Trump's executive order was something other than what the government's lawyers claimed in court. Once more, the big mouths behind Trump and his Administration are helping to defeat their own policies.

Sanctuary Cities Make Us Safer

Raul Reyes

Raul Reyes is an author, attorney, and television commentator based in New York.

Before the July 4 weekend, a tragedy occurred in San Francisco. Kate Steinle, 32, was walking with her father on a busy pier when she was allegedly shot and killed by Juan Francisco Lopez-Sanchez, an undocumented immigrant from Mexico with a long rap sheet.

The randomness of this crime shocked the nation, and led to a renewed debate over so-called sanctuary cities like San Francisco. Several of the leading Republican candidates for president, including Donald Trump, Jeb Bush and Rand Paul, have since weighed in against sanctuary cities.

Not so fast. "Sanctuary cities" is a misleading label that has caused a great deal of confusion. The term is a misnomer for those cities and towns that prefer that the federal government handle immigration enforcement. It is wrong to attack sanctuary cities: Their policies actually help make our cities and towns safer.

A sanctuary city is a city that has decided to leave immigration enforcement to the federal government so that its own police force can concentrate on fighting crime. That's hardly a radical idea; it is a principle that the Supreme Court affirmed in *Arizona v. U.S.* (2012), which found that only the federal government had authority over immigration enforcement.

There are several hundred sanctuary cities across the country, including Los Angeles, New York, San Francisco and Seattle. Although the policies of sanctuary cities vary from place to place, it might surprise people to know that sanctuary cities do not provide a haven for undocumented immigrants. Federal immigration laws

"Sanctuary Cities Actually Make Us Safer," by Raul A. Reyes, *The Hartford Courant*, August 4, 2015. Reprinted by permission.

are enforced in sanctuary cities just as in non-sanctuary cities. In a sanctuary city, undocumented immigrants can still be rounded up and deported by the government. Local officials in sanctuary cities can still report undocumented immigrants to the government.

One way to understand why sanctuary cities are a smart idea is to look at their history. Starting in the 1990s, when illegal immigration was on the rise, the federal government rolled out several programs whereby local law enforcement would assist them in catching and removing undocumented immigrants. As it turned out, local police didn't want to do this—and with good reason.

State and local police are not trained in immigration law and procedures. Holding undocumented immigrants in local jails proved to be very expensive for cities, and led to additional liability and legal issues. Local police forces found that they didn't have enough time to do their main job, protecting their communities from crime, because they were chasing after people for immigration violations, which are civil infractions.

Worst of all, when local police were turned into immigration agents, it had a detrimental effect on community relations. A 2013 study by the University of Illinois-Chicago found that increased (local) police involvement in immigration enforcement eroded trust of law enforcement among both undocumented and legal immigrants.

As a result of this confusion and pushback, cities turned to sanctuary policies, which in effect tells the federal government: You do your job, we'll do ours.

Sanctuary cities are doing something right. Crime in San Francisco, for example, is lower than in several other non-sanctuary cities. Sanctuary cities make sense because they allow undocumented immigrants to report crime and volunteer as witnesses with local police, which makes everyone safer. Consider that a long list of cities, mayors, crime victims and law enforcement groups have spoken out against a proposal by House Republicans to withhold federal funds from sanctuary cities.

Steinle's death was a horrific crime and her killer must be brought to justice. But we shouldn't let an emotional response to this crime blind us to the realities of the case. Steinle's death occurred because of a bureaucratic error; given his criminal history, Lopez-Sanchez should never have been released by San Francisco police.

Similarly, a Haitian immigrant in Connecticut allegedly fatally stabbed a woman when he should have already been deported. "If our federal agencies had been on top of this, my daughter would still be here with us," her mother told a Connecticut paper. But immigration authorities tried repeatedly to deport the alleged killer to Haiti. They were hampered by the fact that Haiti refused to accept him back—not by a sanctuary city policy.

So instead of scapegoating sanctuary cities, lawmakers should be taking steps to ensure better communication between federal and local law enforcement. Besides, we don't need more immigration enforcement (our government spends more on immigration enforcement than all other federal law enforcement agencies combined); we need smarter and better immigration enforcement. One step in the right direction is the recent news that the Obama administration will be focusing its immigration enforcement efforts on convicted felons, recent arrivals and security/terrorist threats. Until our country tackles comprehensive immigration reform, sanctuary cities make our cities safer. It is misguided, uninformed and myopic to attack them as bad policy.

Police Chiefs Support Sanctuary Cities Because They Keep Crime Down

Chuck Wexler

Chuck Wexler is the executive director of the Police Executive Research Forum, which works with police departments to improve the policing profession.

With an estimated 11 million undocumented people living in the United States, talk of a crackdown on illegal immigration has created tension in cities across the country.

For America's police chiefs, calls for enhanced enforcement of federal immigration laws bring a particular concern. Chiefs are afraid that such efforts will have the unintended consequence of actually increasing crime and making their communities less safe. The reasons for this can be found in recent incidents from some of the country's so-called sanctuary cities.

In Tucson, for example, an undocumented man confronted and physically struggled with a man who tried to steal a car with children inside. The immigrant held the criminal long enough for local police to arrive, then cooperated with detectives in the follow-up investigation. As a result, the suspect was charged with kidnapping, auto theft and burglary.

In Laredo, Texas, Sister Rosemary Welsh runs Casa de Misericordia, which provides shelter to women, many of whom are undocumented immigrants and victims of domestic violence. Because of the trust Sister Rosemary has built with local law enforcement and the women in her facility, more victims are reporting crime, and more offenders are identified and prosecuted.

Los Angeles, a city with an estimated 375,000 undocumented immigrants, has had a policy prohibiting police from engaging

"Op-Ed: Police chiefs across the country support sanctuary cities because they keep crime down," by Chuck Wexler, Police Executive Research Forum, Los Angeles Times, March 6, 2017. Reprinted by permission.

in enforcement activities based solely on a person's immigration status since 1979. Last year, LAPD officers had an encounter with a suspected gang member that resulted in a vehicle chase, a foot pursuit and shots being fired. An undocumented immigrant helped police locate the suspect by providing a description and vehicle information.

Had these undocumented people, and countless others in cities across America, not stepped forward to report crime and cooperate with the police, we would have more dangerous offenders committing more crime — and more serious crime — against innocent victims.

Police chiefs know that today's unreported domestic violence or sexual assault or robbery can become tomorrow's reported homicide. This is a special concern in immigrant communities, where many people fear that cooperating with the police may lead to scrutiny and even deportation. It's why cities have adopted policies like the one in Los Angeles, and it's why police departments have invested considerable time and resources to build trust and cooperation with all of their communities, including their immigrant communities. They know that when people step forward because they trust their local police, communities are safer.

For all these reasons, the label of sanctuary city is a misnomer. The term "sanctuary" dates to classical Greece and Rome, and to Christian traditions in the Middle Ages. Back then, sanctuaries provided certain protections to fugitives in churches or other sacred locations. The details changed over time, but sanctuary generally consisted of limited, temporary protections to people suspected of certain types of crimes, and only in narrow circumstances.

The use of the term to describe a set of protections for undocumented immigrants implies that they somehow get a pass to commit crime within those jurisdictions. This is simply not the case. It is the mission of all police departments, including those in so-called sanctuary cities, to go after serious and violent criminal offenders for investigation, arrest, and prosecution, regardless of their immigration status.

In reality, sanctuary cities are hardly sanctuaries for any criminals. Because of the trust and cooperation they have developed with undocumented immigrants, police in these cities are often able to identify, arrest and prosecute dangerous offenders who might otherwise still be on the streets victimizing residents — both citizens and undocumented immigrants.

The issues of public safety and immigration are too complex to be captured in a catchphrase, and they are not new. In the decade that our organization has spent exploring the role of local police in immigration issues, police chiefs have consistently reported several key points.

First, the current system of enforcement is a logical division of labor in which all parties know what is expected of them. Federal agencies, such as Immigration and Customs Enforcement (ICE), enforce immigration laws, which are federal statutes. Local police agencies enforce state and local criminal laws. These roles are compatible and complementary.

Second, local police have their hands full — investigating murders, robberies, sexual assaults, burglaries, thefts and other crimes, and working to prevent these and other crimes from occurring. When local police identify a suspect and have probable cause, they make the arrest, without regard to the suspect's immigration status.

Finally, police chiefs warn that if their agencies are required to enforce federal immigration laws, it will hurt their ability to investigate and solve serious crimes in their communities. If people are afraid to have contact with the local police, they will not report crime, serve as witnesses, or tell police what is going on in their neighborhoods. Without information from the community, investigating crime becomes difficult and crime levels rise.

So that we can have a constructive discussion on public safety and immigration, let's retire the tired misnomer "sanctuary cities" once and for all. Let's focus on what it really takes to make our communities safer.

CHAPTER 3

Are Countries Obligated to Allow Legal Residence?

Differences Between Immigration, Asylum, Refugees, and DACA

Obed Manuel and Brianna Stone

Obed Manuel and Brianna Stone are members of the Curious Texas team at the Dallas Morning News. *They report on politics, government, and social justice–related topics.*

As stories of President Donald Trump's enforcement of the zero-tolerance policy have continued rolling in from the U.S.-Mexico border, curiosity about authorized and unauthorized immigration has spiked.

In response, we launched a special edition of our Curious Texas project inviting readers to ask questions about migration between the U.S. and Mexico and life on both sides of the border.

The reader-submitted questions are indicative of the complexity of border and immigration issues. From how the U.S.-Mexico border came to be where it is to today to a breakdown of the nationalities of people attempting to cross into the country — readers had a lot of questions.

Terri Mento of Plano asks, "Exactly how does someone come into the U.S. legally? What are the steps you have to take? What's the cost of the process? How does the lottery system work?"

The truth is that there are a multitude of ways someone may legally request entry to the U.S.

But given the contentious talking points making the rounds, we figured we would take this opportunity to break down the process and explain the difference between refugees, asylees and Deferred Action for Childhood Arrivals recipients.

"What's the difference between legal immigration, asylum, refugees and DACA? Curious Texas explains," by Obed Manuel and Brianna Stone, *The Dallas Morning News,* June 23, 2018. Reprinted by permission.

How Does One Legally Migrate to the U.S.?

"There are very, very limited categories of people who can come legally to the U.S., and it is a quite lengthy and complicated process even if you fit into one of those categories," said Denise Gilman, immigration clinic director at The University of Texas at Austin.

Ways to legally immigrate include seeking asylum or resettlement as a refugee, having employment or through close family ties, Gilman said.

"It's important to note that the family tie category is very limited and only includes close family — no cousins, uncles," Gilman said. "The wait time can be up to 20 years because there are caps. It can cost thousands of dollars for travel costs and attorneys."

Foreigners who qualify, apply and are approved for a green card, also known as a Permanent Resident Card, are allowed to legally live and work in the U.S.

There is also an "immigration lottery," the Diversity Immigrant Visa Program, that randomly selects up to 50,000 people to receive a Permanent Resident Card. These immigrants, who have visas, are from countries with low rates of immigration to the United States.

Since the Immigration and Naturalization Act of 1965, the U.S. immigration system has a large backlog that results in people having to wait years, Gilman said.

"There's always going to be more people who want to come to the U.S. than the caps allow," she said.

After someone legally migrates to the U.S. from another country, the process for becoming a naturalized citizen varies. It depends on the applicant's time as a permanent U.S. resident, how long they've held continuous residence, their marital status, their spouse's citizenship status, a demonstration of "good moral character," and if they served or plan to serve in the military.

After applying, applicants have a physical and get fingerprinted, interview with an official and take an English and civics test. The cost of the naturalization application and biometric service fee is $725 per applicant.

What Does It Mean to Seek Asylum or Resettlement as a Refugee?

As the effects of the Trump administration's controversial zero-tolerance policy reverberate, there are still people reaching the U.S. border and trying to make a case for asylum.

U.S. Attorney General Jeff Sessions ruled out domestic violence and gang violence — two of the key claims made by Central American asylum seekers — as valid reasons for granting asylum.

As we've seen in the past few weeks, that hasn't deterred people, and families have continued showing up at the border despite reports that border agents have reportedly been blocking asylum seekers from stating their cases.

What Is the Difference Between an Asylee and a Refugee?

Asylum and refugee status are both forms of protection the U.S. offers to certain individuals who are unable or unwilling to return to their home country as a result of being persecuted or having fear of being persecuted for their race, religion, nationality, membership in a certain social group or political opinion.

U.S. Citizenship and Immigration Services policies require that refugees must begin the resettlement process in their homeland. They must be referred to the United States Refugee Admissions Program and undergo a multi-step process that often costs a lot of money.

"When you come as a refugee from abroad to the U.S., you have already been recognized as a refugee," Gilman said. "There is a very lengthy screening and interview process, so only a small number of refugees are resettled. This process is almost not being done at all under this administration."

According to the U.S. Department of State website, the U.S. has accepted more than 3.3 million refugees since 1975.

An asylee is a person who meets the definition of a refugee but is already in the U.S. or is attempting to enter the country at a valid point of entry. If granted asylum status, the individual may then request to be resettled as a refugee.

"It is important to note that you cannot seek asylum in your home country," Gilman said. "You have to get to the U.S. Once you get to the border, officials are supposed to process [the person or people], but now many are being turned away."

What Is DACA?

DACA, the Deferred Action for Childhood Arrivals program, was created in 2012 during Barack Obama's presidency as a temporary solution to grant young people who were brought to the U.S. as children two years of deferred action and two-year work permits that are eligible for renewal.

DACA recipients are neither refugees or asylees and do not have legal status in the U.S.

When someone is approved for DACA, they receive a letter detailing the specifics of their two-year deferred action term along with an explanation of what immigration services have decided about their case.

Before someone is granted deferred action, they must first meet several specific requirements:

- They must have been under 31 years old as of June 15, 2012.
- They must have been under 16 years old before coming to the U.S.
- They must have continuously lived in the U.S. since at least June 15, 2007.
- They must have been physically present at the time of the June 15, 2012, DACA announcement and during the application process.
- They could not have had any lawful status on June 15, 2012.
- They must be in high school or graduated or completed a GED or equivalent or been honorably discharged from the U.S. Armed Forces.
- They could not have been convicted of a felony, significant misdemeanor or three or more misdemeanors.

DACA applicants must provide documentation to prove their continuous residence in the United States. These include school records, ownership titles, medical records, utility bills or bank statements.

They must also submit to a background check and a biometrics appointment, where they are fingerprinted. Once approved, recipients receive an I-766 Work Authorization Permit and can apply for a Social Security number.

Last September, Trump called for the program to gradually shut down, but a federal judge ordered that the government must continue accepting DACA renewals until the litigation was resolved. No first-time applications are being accepted.

The program is also the subject of a federal lawsuit filed in May by Texas Attorney General Ken Paxton and six other states that questions the authority of the president to establish it.

According to September 2017 data from the U.S. Citizenship and Immigration Services, there are about 689,800 DACA recipients, with 113,000 (16.4 percent) in Texas. Behind California, Texas is the state with the second-most DACA recipients.

Rights for Immigrants in the United States

Amnesty International

Amnesty International is an NGO focused on human rights. Though it is based in the UK, it deals with injustices around the globe.

In 2017 and 2018, President Trump's administration has implemented immigration policies that have caused catastrophic irreparable harm to thousands of people, have spurned and manifestly violated both US and international law, and appeared to be aimed at the full dismantling of the US asylum system.

Those policies and practices have included, among others: (1) mass illegal pushbacks of asylum-seekers at the US–Mexico border; (2) thousands of illegal family separations, through which the Trump administration has deliberately and purposefully inflicted extreme suffering on families, ill-treatment which rose to the level of torture in some cases; and (3) increasingly arbitrary and indefinite detention of asylum-seekers, without parole, constituting cruel, inhuman or degrading treatment or punishment (ill-treatment) which is absolutely prohibited in international law.

Based on public statements by US government officials, those policies and practices were indisputably intended to deter asylum-seekers from requesting protection in the United States, as well as to punish and compel those who did seek protection to give up their asylum claims.

> They told me, 'you don't have any rights here, and you don't have any rights to stay with your son.' …For me I died at that moment. They ripped my heart out of me. …For me, it would have been better if I had dropped dead. For me, the world ended at that point. …How can a mother not have the right to be with her son?
>
> —*Valquiria, a 39-year-old Brazilian asylum-seeker, detained since March 2018, when US authorities*

"USA: 'You don't have any rights here,'" Amnesty International. Reprinted by permission.

> *forcibly separated her from her 6-year-old son, after they requested asylum at a port-of-entry in El Paso, Texas.*

These are not isolated aberrations. The US Department of Homeland Security (DHS) has implemented these interrelated policies in unison: closing the borders to asylum-seekers, and pushing them back into harm's way; and making life so intolerable in immigration detention facilities, that asylum-seekers would think twice before requesting protection in the United States.

Fuelling these policies of cruelty with discriminatory and demonizing rhetoric, President Trump and his cabinet members have routinely called asylum-seekers "criminals," and denounced international standards on refugee protection as legal "loopholes" and "magic words" that the administration has professed its intention to abolish.

The Trump administration is waging a deliberate campaign of human rights violations against asylum seekers, in order to broadcast globally that the United States no longer welcomes refugees. Simultaneously, the Trump administration is seeking to dismantle the US asylum system, including by narrowing definitions of who qualifies for protection—in violation of international law. Setting a dangerous precedent, the US government's abrogation of its obligations under human rights and refugee law is undermining the international framework for refugee protection, grossly violating the right to seek asylum, and is inviting a race to the bottom by other countries.

Illegal Pushbacks

In 2017 and 2018, despite historic lows in the number of people seeking to enter the US without legal status, including asylum-seekers, the DHS border agency Customs and Border Protection (CBP) has implemented an illegal de facto policy of pushbacks of asylum-seekers along the entire US–Mexico border at official US border crossings (called "ports-of-entry"). Pushbacks of asylum-seekers are both illegal under US law and violate US obligations under international refugee law.

By turning away asylum-seekers at US ports-of-entry, the United States has grossly violated their right to seek asylum from persecution, and manufactured an emergency along the US–Mexico border. US authorities have forced thousands of asylum-seekers to queue on the Mexican side of the border—exposing them to risks of detention and deportation by Mexican immigration officials, and exploitation by criminal gangs. CBP personnel have also regularly turned away Mexican nationals seeking asylum in the United States, including unaccompanied minors.

Those mass pushbacks of asylum-seekers by CBP are plainly unlawful, and violate one of the most fundamental principles of international refugee law: the prohibition on refoulement (forcing people to a place where they might be at risk of serious human rights violations). This principle is incorporated into US law, which requires border and immigration authorities to receive and refer asylum-seekers for an interview with an asylum officer, in order to conduct individual assessments of any risks of persecution or torture that they may face upon return.

Two senior Mexican immigration officials independently informed Amnesty International that US authorities encouraged Mexico to detain and check the legal status of asylum-seekers whom CBP was forcing to wait in Mexico, with a potential view to deporting them to their countries-of-origin. Any such deportations would constitute indirect refoulement in violation of both US and Mexican authorities' legal obligations. Amnesty International documented in two 2017 reports that the asylum-seekers arriving at the US–Mexico border are often in need of protection from persecution including targeted violence in their home countries, after perilous journeys to the southern US border. Many have fled from the Northern Triangle region of Central America (El Salvador, Guatemala and Honduras), where Amnesty International has documented human rights violations often waged against civilians by or with the acquiescence of their own governments.

The Trump administration has leveraged vague claims of "capacity" constraints, as an escape hatch to violate its legal obligations to receive and process asylum-seekers' requests for protection. There appears to be no official written or other record of interactions between CBP officers and asylum-seekers when CBP denies them the opportunity to claim asylum at US ports-of-entry. Yet CBP's actions have been public, consistent and synchronized at widely dispersed ports-of-entry, despite variations in the numbers of asylum-seekers requesting protection at each crossing.

In parallel to its systematic campaign of illegal pushbacks along the US–Mexico border, the US government has sought to negotiate a "safe third country agreement" with Mexico. Under such an agreement, the United States would recognize Mexico as a safe destination country for all asylum seekers, and stop accepting asylum claims at the US–Mexico border, except from those fearing persecution in Mexico itself.

Under both US and international law, however, the United States cannot legally adopt a "safe third country agreement" with Mexico, since it is not a uniformly safe country for all asylum-seekers. Amnesty International has documented Mexican immigration officials routinely deporting asylum-seekers to potential persecution in their countries-of-origin, in violation of Mexican and international law. Under US law, DHS authorities therefore must continue to receive and provide individualized and fair assessments of all requests for protection by asylum-seekers at US borders and on US territory.

Family Separations

In November 2017 in California, DHS officials tore apart four Central American families at once in the same room: "You don't have any rights here," a DHS officer told an asylum-seeking father from El Salvador, when he protested the handcuffing of his 12-year-old son. In March 2018 in Texas, a DHS officer said the same phrase to an asylum-seeking mother from Brazil, while separating her from her son: "You don't have any rights here. And you don't have any rights to stay with your son." Both of those families had documents proving their family relationships, and presented themselves at official US ports of entry when requesting asylum from persecution in their countries-of-origin.

At first tested discretely in 2017, and then launched publicly in 2018, President Trump's administration implemented a policy of forcibly separating thousands of asylum-seeking families, in order to deter and punish those crossing irregularly into the United States. Under its so-called "zero-tolerance" policy, the US government claimed that family separations were a necessary result of criminally prosecuting all asylum-seekers and others who crossed the US–Mexico border irregularly (i.e. between official ports-of-entry). In reality, US authorities also separated many asylum-seekers who were not referred for criminal prosecution—including those who sought protection at official border crossings—yet has continued to deny and conceal the practice.

The US government has still not publicly disclosed the total number of families it forcibly separated in 2017 and 2018. In September 2018, however, CBP provided statistics to Amnesty International suggesting that the Trump administration separated approximately 8,000 "family units"—more than US authorities had previously admitted to separating. Those statistics still seemed to omit hundreds—if not thousands—of families separated at official ports-of-entry, or with non-parental relationships (including grandparents, among others).

In 2018, Amnesty International interviewed 15 asylum-seekers whom DHS agencies separated from their children, both prior to and following the introduction of the so-called "zero-tolerance" policy. Most of these families were separated without being informed of why, and despite having documentary evidence of their family relationships. In 13 of the 15 cases, DHS separated the families after they requested protection at official US ports-of-entry. When they spoke with Amnesty International, some of the separated parents and guardians were suffering from such extreme mental anguish that they wept uncontrollably as they recounted their experiences, sometimes only seconds or minutes into interviews. Amnesty International researchers witnessed the extreme mental anguish those family separations caused, as well as instances of family separation being leveraged to compel a family to abandon their asylum claim. In some of the cases documented by Amnesty International, the harmful practice of family separations satisfied the definitions of torture under US and international law.

"I believe that because of all of this I'm going through—the fear of going back to Brazil, the fear of being separated from my grandchild, all of this together, I can't stop thinking about it—that it's making me really sick," said Maria (55), who was separated from her grandson with disabilities, Matheus (17), after they requested asylum in New Mexico in August 2017. "I might need to go look for a psychologist. I don't remember things, and can't sleep…I start to talk about something and forget what I was saying. I am crying a lot also because I am still separated from Matheus." Family separations violate multiple fundamental human rights at once, including the right to family unity, the right to liberty, and the right to freedom from torture and other ill-treatment. Both the prosecution of asylum-seekers for irregular entry, and the forcible separation of their families, also violated US obligations under international refugee law. Children's rights are also violated in multiple ways through family separations, including by exposing them to extreme and unnecessary trauma after being separated. In the cases documented by Amnesty International, it was clear that authorities did not consider children's best interests when separating them from their families.

Arbitrary and Indefinite Detention

In 2017 and 2018, the US government has implemented an official policy of mandatory and indefinite detention of asylum-seekers, without parole, for the duration of their asylum claims.

The policy and practice of indefinitely detaining asylum-seekers, based solely on their migration status, constitute arbitrary detention in violation of US and international law. Indefinite detention without criminal charge is in violation of the UN

Convention Against Torture, which the United States ratified and integrated into US law.

> I applied for parole, with all the documentation requested, but the request was denied. ...I was not told the reason they denied my parole, just that it was denied. None of us have been given parole.
>
> —*Alejandra, a 43-year-old transgender rights activist from El Salvador, detained by ICE since December 2017 at the Cibola County Correctional Center in New Mexico. ICE denied her parole three times in 2018, without justification.*

Intended to deter and punish those who seek protection at the US–Mexico border, the US government expanded the use of indefinite detention of asylum-seekers both through blanket denials of parole requests by asylum-seekers in some regions, which a US federal court in July 2018 found likely to be arbitrary and illegal; and through its family separations policy, by which it detained parents individually without their children.

The US government has also sought legal authority to indefinitely detain unaccompanied children and families with children, despite it being unlawful in the United States and contrary to international standards.

US authorities have leveraged the agony of prolonged detention in order to compel asylum-seekers to "voluntarily" give up their asylum claims, and accept deportation back to their countries-of-origin where they had fled persecution. That anguish of indefinite detention has often been amplified by family separations and inadequate conditions of detention, including routinely substandard health care that has contributed in some cases to asylum-seekers' deaths in immigration detention facilities.

In three of the four US states bordering Mexico, Amnesty International interviewed asylum-seekers being detained indefinitely after requesting protection, including separated family members, older people, and persons with acute health conditions and medical needs. Amnesty International also documented the impact of arbitrary immigration detention on 15 transgender and gay asylum-seekers, who were detained for periods ranging from several months to over 2.5 years without parole. In some cases those individuals were denied parole despite acute health conditions and needs for specialized care, or following sexual assaults while in detention. Compounded by past trauma, substandard health care, and reportedly inadequate physical conditions, food and water, as well as discrimination based on sexual orientation, gender identity and/or ethnicity, Amnesty International found some of those asylum-seekers' experiences of indefinite detention had constituted ill-treatment.

Methodology

In 2017 and 2018, Amnesty International conducted extensive baseline research on the situation of asylum-seekers in the United States and on the US–Mexico border, including through the review of legal files, review of national and international legal standards, and consultations with relevant civil society groups.

In January, April and May 2018, Amnesty International researchers conducted research missions along the entire US–Mexico border, from the Pacific Ocean to the Gulf of Mexico. The research teams documented not only the situations of asylum-seekers who sought to request protection at US ports-of-entry, but also the conduct of US border and immigration authorities in facilitating and processing their asylum claims under US law and international law and standards.

Amnesty International researchers interviewed a total of 52 asylum-seekers along the US–Mexico border, including in all four US border states (California, Arizona, New Mexico, and Texas) and three Mexican border states (Baja California, Sonora, and Chihuahua). Among those 52 asylum-seekers were 27 men and 25 women, including 15 transgender women. Amnesty International interviewed 28 asylum-seekers inside ICE immigration detention facilities (in California, New Mexico, and Texas); 14 asylum-seekers in Mexico, including 12 who were turned away and two who were removed by the United States to Mexico; three asylum-seekers who were on parole at the time of the interview; and seven refugees who had been granted asylum.

Amnesty International also interviewed 51 immigration lawyers, activists and other representatives of nongovernmental organizations (NGOs); as well as 23 government and other officials. Among those officials were 12 representatives of CBP or ICE, three US subcontractors at private detention facilities; six Mexican immigration officials; and two Mexican municipal government officials. Throughout 2018, Amnesty International conducted extensive follow-up research to corroborate first-hand accounts of asylum-seekers, through review of court documentation, legal filings and other official records, wherever possible, as well as follow-up correspondence and interviews with government officials, lawyers, and NGOs.

Key Recommendations

To the US Congress

- Exercise greater oversight of DHS agencies to: halt the illegal pushbacks of asylum-seekers at US ports-of-entry; curtail any executive overreach, especially this administration's attempts to separate and/or indefinitely detain asylum-seeking families and children; and end the arbitrary and indefinite detention of asylum-seekers, in violation of international law.
- Increase funding for immigration judges, and USCIS asylum and refugee officers.
- Pass legislation banning the separation and/or detention of families with children.
- Support and fund community-based alternatives to detention, such as the previous Family Case Management Program.
- Decriminalize irregular entry into the United States, in line with international standards, and ensure that administrative sanctions applied to irregular entry are proportionate and reasonable.

- Ratify the UN Convention on the Rights of the Child, which the United States signed in 1995 and is the only country in the world not to adopt.

To the US Department of Homeland Security

Illegal Pushbacks

- Immediately stop turning away asylum-seekers at the US–Mexico border, both at and between official ports-of-entry.
- Discontinue all plans and actions that would require asylum-seekers at the US–Mexico border to wait in Mexico during pendency of their asylum claims.

Family Separations and Detention

- End detention of children, whether accompanied or unaccompanied, separated or held together with their family, as it is never in their best interest.
- Reunify, unconditionally, as quickly as possible and sparing no costs, any and all children who remain separated from their parents or guardians.
- Halt family separations in all circumstances, except following a rigorous determination of best interests of the child, which must be articulated to family members and recorded in the case files of those affected.
- Strengthen mechanisms and procedures to ensure that the separation of children of asylum-seekers and migrants occurs only when it is in their best interest, including improved safeguards for the determination of those best interests.

Detention of Asylum-Seekers

- Ensure that liberty is the default position, and that the detention of asylum-seekers and other people is exceptional and only resorted to when it is determined to be necessary and proportionate to a legitimate purpose, based on an assessment of the individual's particular circumstances.

- Resume and expand alternative-to-detention programs for all asylum-seekers, and particularly asylum-seeking families, including the Family Case Management Program.

To the US Department of Justice

- In line with US obligations under the international human rights treaties to which it is party: prohibit the practice of family separations; initiate a criminal investigation into the practice, and the harm it has caused to those subjected to it; hold accountable all those who authorized the practice; and grant compensation and other reparations to families who were separated, in order to ensure their rehabilitation, with specific attention to the needs of children.
- Abandon efforts to recognize Mexico as a safe country for all asylum-seekers, in violation of US and international law.

New Immigration Rules Would End Current Asylum Protections

Julian Borger

Julian Borger is the world affairs editor at the Guardian UK. *Previously he was a foreign correspondent and author of* The Butcher's Trail.

The Trump administration has announced new immigration rules ending asylum protections for almost all migrants who arrive at the US-Mexico border, in violation of both US and international law.

According to the new rules, any asylum seekers who pass through another country before arriving at the southern border—including children traveling on their own—will not be eligible for asylum if they failed to apply first in their country of transit. They would only be eligible for US asylum if their application was turned down elsewhere.

The change would affect the vast majority of migrants arriving through Mexico. Most of those currently come from Guatemala, Honduras and El Salvador, but an increasing number are from Haiti, Cuba and countries further afield in Africa and Asia.

The new rules were placed on the federal register on Monday and due to take effect on Tuesday, though they will be immediately challenged in court for contraventions of the US refugee act and the UN refugee convention guaranteeing the right to seek asylum to those fleeing persecution from around the world.

Filippo Grandi, the UN high commissioner for refugees, said he was deeply concerned by the move. "It will put vulnerable families at risk. It will undermine efforts by countries across the region to devise the coherent, collective responses that are needed. This measure is severe and is not the best way forward," he said.

"Trump's 'blatantly illegal' immigration rules end asylum protections," by Julian Borger, Guardian News and Media Limited, July 15, 2019. Reprinted by permission.

The American Civil Liberties Union said the rules were "patently unlawful" and said it would sue the administration to block them taking effect.

In a joint statement, the Departments of Homeland Security and Justice said the rules "add a new bar to eligibility for asylum" for migrants arriving at the southern border "who did not apply for protection from persecution or torture where it was available in at least one third country outside the alien's country of citizenship, nationality or last lawful habitual residence."

The attorney general, William Barr, said: "This rule will decrease forum shopping by economic migrants and those who seek to exploit our asylum system to obtain entry to the United States, while ensuring that no one is removed from the United States who is more likely than not to be tortured or persecuted on account of a protected ground."

The US Refugee Act of 1980 limits the right of asylum if the applicant can be sent back to a "safe third country," but human rights advocates have pointed out that neither Mexico nor any Central American countries come close to meeting the act's standards of a safe third country, "where the alien's life or freedom would not be threatened"... "and where the alien would have access to a full an fair procedure for determining a claim to asylum."

Furthermore, for a country to be considered "safe," it would have to enter into a formal agreement with the US. In recent months, the US has sought to conclude safe third country agreements with Mexico and Guatemala, but Mexico rejected the initiative and the agreement in Guatemala was blocked on Sunday by that country's constitutional court. The new rules published on Monday simply ignore the safe third country standard.

Mexico continued to express muted support for asylum seekers, even as the country cracks down on migrants crossing its southern border.

The foreign minister, Marcelo Ebrard, said that the new rules would not apply to Mexicans or turn Mexico into a safe third country. "Mexico doesn't agree with measures that limits people seeking asylum or refuge," he said.

The move represents the latest in a series of steps the Trump administration has taken to cut off the flow of migrants through the US-Mexico border. Under the "migrant protection protocols," the US has required migrants to wait in Mexico while their cases are decided in US immigration courts.

"The Trump administration is yet again attempting to rewrite and violate laws passed by Congress to protect refugees from return to persecution," said Eleanor Acer, the director of refugee protection at Human Rights First. "This new rule is dangerous, disgraceful and blatantly illegal."

"This rule will be challenged because it is contrary to the asylum statute and to US obligations to refugees under international law," Keren Zwick, a litigator at the National Immigrant Justice Centre.

An Amnesty International assessment of the Mexican asylum system found it was "underfunded, absolutely beyond its capacity and inadequate in identifying even valued asylum claims" according to the organisation's advocacy director for the Americas, Charanya Krishnaswami. The study found that Mexico sent a quarter of applicants back to the countries they were fleeing without due process.

"Those dangers make clear that Mexico would not be a safe place for the many thousands who are seeking protection at the US border," Krishnaswami said.

Moral Considerations for Immigration

Mathias Risse

Mathias Risse is a professor of philosophy and public administration in the John F. Kennedy School of Government at Harvard University, where he is also director of the Carr Center for Human Rights Policy.

My goal here is twofold: First, I wish to make a plea for the relevance of moral considerations in debates about immigration. Too often, immigration debates are conducted solely from the standpoint of "what is good for us," without regard for the justifiability of immigration policies to those excluded. Second, I wish to offer a standpoint that demonstrates why one should think of immigration as a moral problem that must be considered in the context of global justice. More specifically, I will argue that the earth belongs to humanity in common and that this matters for assessing immigration policy. The case I will be particularly interested in is immigration into the United States, where immigration policy continues to be a hotly debated topic. However, that discussion takes the form of a case study: the relevant considerations apply generally.

To give some initial grounding to the standpoint that the earth belongs to humanity in common, let us suppose for the sake of argument that the population of the United States shrinks to two, but that these two can control access into the country through sophisticated electronic border-surveillance mechanisms. Suppose, too, that nothing changes in the rest of the world. I would argue (and I think most would agree) that under such conditions these two citizens should allow for immigration based on the fact that they are grossly underusing the territory under their control. If this is so, then it follows that what we do with the space we control must matter for assessing immigration policy. It further follows in

Risse, M. (2008). "On the Morality of Immigration." Ethics & International Affairs, 22(1), 25-33 © Carnegie Council for Ethics in International Affairs 2008, published by Cambridge University Press. Reproduced with permission.

particular that, given that by global standards the population of the United States is too small relative to the amount of space to which it claims exclusive control, illegal immigrants should be naturalized and more widespread immigration should be permitted.

Questions about immigration fundamentally challenge those who see themselves in the liberal camp. One hallmark of the liberal state is that it takes individual attitudes in many areas of life as given and rules them out only if they threaten the functionality of the state. When confronted with immigration, a liberal state may choose to develop a systematic approach, and thus come up with a view of what kind of people it wants to include or exclude, or it may choose not to develop such an approach. In the first case the liberal state passes judgment on people in terms of their fitness for membership. Any criterion used for inclusion also reflects a judgment on those who already live in the country, and will bring about change that is beneficial for some citizens and detrimental for others. In the second case the liberal state has to live with the consequences of whatever alternative approach it develops.

Things become yet more complicated if one sees immigration in a global context. Immigration can plausibly be regarded as one way of satisfying duties toward the global poor—duties that many political leaders and citizens, as well as most contemporary philosophers, would acknowledge, at least in some form. Immigration—permanent or temporary—can serve this function partly because it allows some people access to greener pastures, and partly because of the remittances sent back by immigrants to their countries of origin. Once we think of immigration in a global context, we are led to ask more fundamental questions— namely, why it would be acceptable in the first place (especially to those thus excluded) that we draw an imaginary line in the dust or adopt the course of a river and think of that *as a border.* As Rousseau famously remarks at the opening of Part II of his *Second Discourse on Inequality,* "The first person who, having fenced off a lot of ground, took it into his head to say *this is mine* and found people simple enough to believe him, was the true founder of civil society." Is it only because of such simplicity that states are accepted? Such thoughts leave us wondering about the legitimacy of a system of states per se.

The Moral Questions

We have now brought into focus one immense difficulty of discussing questions about immigration: it easily involves one in major moral questions. Thus, what one can sensibly say about questions that arise in the context of immigration policy turns on what parameters one considers fixed for the purposes of the debate. Discussions about immigration, more than most other political issues, easily become frustrating because people intuitively differ over how much political background structure should be kept fixed, and because it is often questionable at what stage one should say that a certain proposal is untenable because "ought implies can"—that is, there is no point in exploring a certain proposal because it is clearly not politically feasible.

Of course, in the realm of the political, what can be done depends largely on what one can convince or persuade others to approve. The limits of what is politically doable are themselves, at least to a large extent, shaped by political debate. The idea that a fence should be built along the U.S. border with Mexico clearly is not off limits, in the sense that the "ought implies can" restriction cannot be applied; indeed, the proposal has been discussed. What, then, about the idea that the United States should introduce mandatory identification cards that would include a sophisticated registration system, making it easier to track people? Or the idea that the number of border patrol officers should be increased by a factor of twenty? Or the idea that new immigrants should receive $100,000 in start-up support because their ancestors, unlike those of longer-term citizens, have not had the opportunity to position themselves in the American economy? Or the idea that there should be no borders to begin with?

Depending on which of these ideas one considers feasible, debates about immigration look rather different, and in such debates people often talk past each other because of unarticulated disagreements precisely about what can be under consideration and what cannot. Difficulties of this sort confront us more fully when it comes to assessing illegal immigration. How should we think about illegal immigrants? First of all, are they actually doing something wrong? True, they are breaking the law, but, arguably, from a moral standpoint not all ways of breaking the law are to be condemned.

If one subscribes to the belief that there should be constraints on the sovereignty of any given state, it is no longer obvious that anything is morally wrong with illegal immigration per se. Specifically, if a country limits immigration in a manner that goes beyond what it is morally entitled to, illegal immigration is a legitimate response. One important way in which sovereignty should be constrained emerges from the idea that humanity as a whole owns the earth and its resources in common—not, of course, all those things that in some sense are man-made, but the original resources of the earth. After all—and this is the intuitive argument for this standpoint—such resources are needed by all, and their existence is the accomplishment of no one. Indeed, much of the political philosophy of the seventeenth century was guided by the idea that the earth collectively belongs to humanity, a thought that mattered tremendously to European intellectuals of the time in assessing what sort of claims fledgling colonial powers could make to other parts of the world. Hugo Grotius's *De Jure Belli ac Pacis* was written entirely from a standpoint of collective ownership, and related ideas were also central to Locke, Pufendorf, Selden, Filmer, and even Hobbes.

In addition to the question of immigration, an obvious topic that would benefit from revitalizing the standpoint of collective ownership is climate change. More generally, humankind now confronts numerous problems that are of global import, and that in fact affect the future of the planet itself. Revitalizing the standpoint of collective ownership could be beneficial to thinking about such problems. In the seventeenth century the motivation behind this approach was largely theological, taking as its point of departure the biblical dictum that God gave the earth to humankind in common. But as I hope to demonstrate here, the basic idea can be made plausible without reference to such theological foundations.

The point of thinking about the earth as collectively *owned* is not to establish human despotism over the rest of the earth, organic or inorganic, but to emphasize that all human beings, no matter when and where they were born, are in some sense symmetrically located with regard to the earth's resources and cannot be arbitrarily excluded from them by accidents of space and time. There are different ways of interpreting this idea that humanity owns the earth in common. It might mean that everyone has a claim to an equal share of the planet's overall resources; or that a collective process is needed to satisfy each co-owner as far as any use of the resources is concerned; or that the earth as a whole is like the town commons of old, where each co-owner had a right of use within certain constraints. These different views are all interpretations or conceptions of a more generic view that I call *Egalitarian Ownership*, and I would argue that this is the most plausible view of the ownership of natural resources.

Libertarians like to belittle this view, and have asked whether, say, a nugget of gold found on the ocean floor then belongs to all of humanity, and precisely what that would mean for dividing up its value. But none of these different ways of spelling out Egalitarian Ownership applies ideas of collective ownership object by object. What matters is that each person has an equal share of the world's resources *overall*.

Perhaps people born into a given society should not be favored in terms of access to its achievements. Yet an argument for that view would differ from the one presented here, which is concerned only with the earth's natural conditions and resources. True, the distinction between what "is just there" and what has been shaped by humans has become blurred, given that humans have wrested land from the sea, natural gas from garbage deposits, and so forth. But by and large we understand well enough the idea of what exists without human interference. Formulating this general viewpoint of common ownership of the earth is rather straightforward, but much philosophical energy could and would have to be spent to develop it more carefully. In particular, such energy would be required to determine why one of these conceptions of Egalitarian Ownership should be considered superior to the others, and precisely how we should delineate between the heaps of stuff that are collectively owned and those to which there are special entitlements.[1]

This article is not the place to go into these challenges, but one implication of the best understanding of Egalitarian Ownership is that organized groups of people are justified in excluding others from the space they occupy *only if* that space is populated by sufficiently many people. Specifically, "sufficiently many people" describes when the number of people already occupying that space is proportionate to the value for human purposes of the resources thereby taken out of general use. For current purposes we can take as the reference point of these proportionality judgments the average population-to-space ratio across territorial states. If that ratio is smaller than the world average, it means that any given unit of resources is used by fewer people in that territorial state than the average unit of resources across the world; or, equivalently, it means that any given person in that territorial state has access to more resources than people on average do.

Yet while this, too, is a simple thought to formulate, it is surprisingly hard to spell out; for instance, one needs to wonder about exactly what counts as "use" in the relevant sense (surely not just what is in actual circulation but also, say, what is accessibly in the ground but not yet in circulation). After all, assessing what number of people would be ideally proportionate to the value for human purposes of certain resources is not just a matter of population density, which assesses such proportionality in terms of the sheer size of a territory. Territories of the same size might differ significantly in terms of available resources as well as soil quality, climatic conditions, and other influencing variables. In short, there is a host of biophysical factors that shapes the value of a territory for human purposes, as do current technological constraints.

Much of the empirical work needed to make the relevant valuing operation precise is currently unavailable. That, of course, does not mean that something like this cannot be done in a plausible manner, but so far there has simply not been sufficient interest in thinking about immigration and other questions from this standpoint. Nevertheless, one should not be too dismissive of this standpoint, and certainly not because we do not currently have all the empirical insights available to think it through conclusively.

By the Numbers

Again, the relevant measure of proportionate use is decidedly not population density, but for now let us use it anyway as only a very rough guide. Doing so makes it plausible to say that the United States is severely underusing its chunk of three-dimensional, commonly owned space. Germany has a population density of about 600 per square mile, as does the United Kingdom. For Japan it is 830, for the Netherlands 1,200, and for Bangladesh 2,600. In the United States overall it is 80 per square mile. Of course, population density varies by state, but only in Massachusetts, Rhode Island, and New Jersey does this number rise above 800, and in no state is it much above 1,100. In cities it is yet different: New York City has about 26,000 inhabitants per square mile, and eight other U.S. cities are above 7,500. London has about 11,000, Tokyo 33,000, and Paris 52,000 people per square mile. In light of these numbers, it is amusing that in debates about immigration many Americans think that there are already too many people living in their country.

Of course, extensive policy changes would be needed to accommodate large numbers of new immigrants, but if one just looks at these numbers, one gets the impression that the United States is critically underusing the resources under its control. If this impression is correct, then there can be nothing much wrong with illegal immigration. It would then be a matter of domestic policy to set appropriate incentives so that the incoming population did not all settle in the same locations, such as in a few large cities. This might be similar to the incentives set by the Canadian government for people to settle in the more northern parts of the country. Notice that this standpoint does not argue in support of generally open borders. But what it does say is that as long as a country underuses its resources and refuses to permit more immigration in response, illegal immigration cannot be morally condemned.

One might argue that even though illegal immigration would not be morally wrong from the standpoint of common ownership of the earth, other considerations matter as well for its possible wrongness, the most obvious being that the laws of a morally acceptable state should be respected even when the state simply qua law, and not necessarily because the law is morally supportable, only address those who are already members of the respective society. To those people one could say that perhaps their ongoing presence in a given country or their active participation in certain parts of its economic, social, or political life provides a tacit acceptance of the law of the land and gives them a reason to obey the law—even in cases where it does go morally astray. Perhaps a kind of fair-play argument might be applied, or perhaps some of these people, like naturalized citizens, have even given explicit consent to abide by the laws. But none of this would give would-be illegal immigrants a reason not to break that particular law, and thus none of this would demonstrate to them that they are doing anything morally wrong—provided they merely wished to become regular participants in society and to abide by its laws from then on.

To speak of the United States specifically, one might also argue that the opposition to illegal immigration is based on commonly accepted notions of fairness—including the notion of due process—which loom large in the American psyche. For example, searches on Google using the keywords "wrong," "illegal," and "immigration" delivered a number of American websites on which the unfairness of illegal immigration was emphasized. Illegal immigration makes a mockery of those who abide by the rules, so this argument goes. To pardon illegal immigrants would be unfair because it lets them get away with their offense on the basis that they have succeeded thus far. This standpoint, however, presupposes that immigration is indeed a matter for the respective country alone to sort out, and that the "insiders" are entitled to determine how many and exactly who enters their country. But the argument offered here implies that this is not so. If would-be immigrants are being illegitimately excluded, one cannot complain that they are violating due process if they come anyway.

For those who enter the country illegally with the intention of remaining, common ownership of the earth also suggests a particular argument on their behalf that is inspired by a legal term: the notion of "adverse possession." This term refers to the open occupation of a property (say a house) by people who do not own it, assuming that the situation is known to and not challenged by the actual owner. If this situation persists for a stated period, civil law allows for the ownership to be transferred to the occupying party. Like the absent home owner, the United States underoccupies its claimed space, but it has also created an economic niche for illegal immigrants who know that, often enough, they will find employment, including employment in parts of the economy where illegal immigrants are especially welcome. Since, in addition, the United States falls short of what in principle it *could* do by way of enforcing its immigration law, we can plausibly say that a certain population moves into the country in a rather open manner, and in a manner known to the American society.

True, the immigration status of certain individuals will not be known to certain Americans involved with them, including officials, but in the aggregate, illegal immigration occurs in a manner and on a scale that can plausibly be said to be open and known to the American public and government. Illegal immigrants hold jobs, have driver's licenses, and participate in the life of society in many ways—and again, all of this is known and little is done about it. Thus, while this situation does not have the civil law basis of "adverse possession," clearly a moral form of adverse possession has taken hold.

Conclusion

One might object that, if one implements the political implications of this perspective on immigration, the state could no longer accomplish certain goals to whose realization legitimate states may well be committed. Such goals might include the preservation of a certain culture or its purity, a certain economic or technological standing (human and physical capital and know-how; a wage structure that can be preserved only by regulating labor markets), or a political system (where, for example, modest inequality may depend on keeping the numbers of unskilled workers low). While often such arguments are based on little more than self-interest, we may reinterpret them in their most morally plausible lights as insisting that there is some independent value to realizing these goals.

Yet it is precisely concerns about the reach of such arguments that motivate inquiries into the implications of this standpoint in the first place. A culture shared only by two people occupying a vast territory (such as envisaged earlier) might be eminently worth preserving, but such occupancy would not count as appropriate use from the common-ownership standpoint. The burden of proof is on those who wish to overrule implications of the common-ownership standpoint by granting certain cultures more resources than proportionally they ought to have.

In sum, I have argued that moral considerations should influence immigration policies much more than they currently do. It would be wrong to dismiss this discussion as irrelevant to politics—that is, by suggesting that no one cares about this standpoint of common ownership. As I believe I have demonstrated, it is plausible to arrive naturally at this standpoint, and those engaged in the immigration debate, particularly in the United States, can, I believe, use it to promote attitudes that go beyond simply "what is best for us." Everyday discourse about immigration is in need of reform, and inserting this moral perspective will go some way toward achieving that goal.

Notes

1 Such elaboration is available in "Migration, Territoriality, and Culture" (coauthored with Michael Blake), in *New Waves in Applied Ethics*, Jesper Ryberg, Thomas S. Petersen, and Clark Wolf, eds. (New York: Palgrave Macmillan, 2008); as well as in Michael Blake and Mathias Risse, "Is There a Human Right to Free Movement? Immigration and Original Ownership of the Earth" (forthcoming; available as Kennedy School of Government Faculty Research Working Paper Series RWP06-012).

Asylum for Persecuted Refugees Only

Hans A. von Spakovsky

Hans A. von Spakovsky is a former member of the Federal Election Committee and an attorney. He is now a writer and manager at the Heritage Foundation.

A caravan of more than 7,000 Central Americans is descending on the United States. Like millions of foreigners, they want to live in the U.S. But these people are doing it their way—refusing to participate in our extensive *legal* immigration process.

Most will probably attempt to claim asylum when they get to the border. None should get it, for multiple reasons.

Under federal law (8 U.S.C. 1101(a)(42)), to be granted asylum, an alien must prove that he faces persecution, or has a "well-founded fear of persecution," in his native country "on account of race, religion, nationality, membership in a particular social group, or political opinion." Yet media interviews with those marching toward the border leave little doubt that the vast majority are coming for economic reasons. That doesn't fit within the statutory requirement for asylum.

While asylum *may* be granted to those fleeing persecution, the applicable immigration statute (8 U.S.C. 1158(b)) doesn't require it. Rather, that decision is left to the discretion of the attorney general or the secretary of homeland security.

Attorney General Jeff Sessions pointed this out in a June immigration decision involving an illegal alien from El Salvador who sought asylum in 2014. "Asylum is a discretionary form of relief from removal," Sessions noted, "and an applicant bears the burden of proving not only statutory eligibility for asylum but that she also merits asylum as a matter of discretion." In fact, immigration law directs that the official determining whether an

"No Asylum. Period." by Hans A. von Spakovsky, The Heritage Foundation, October 29, 2018. Reprinted by permission.

alien is entitled to asylum make a "credibility determination" about the alien's claim.

This is important because people often make false asylum claims to get into the country, then disappear into the heartland with no intention of ever showing up for their hearing.

None of those in this latest wave of caravaners—including those who might meet the "persecution" requirement—has sufficient basis for a discretionary grant of asylum. In footnote 12 of his June opinion, Sessions reminds all "asylum adjudicators" that a "relevant discretionary" factor in deciding to grant asylum is whether the alien, while en route to the U.S., "passed through any other countries" where they could have asserted asylum. Were there "orderly refugee procedures…in fact available to help her in any country she passed through" and did the alien make "any attempts to seek asylum before coming to the United States[?]"

It's a crucial question—and one fully in keeping with the procedures of the European Union, which pro-amnesty advocates love to cite as an enlightened entity. The Dublin Regulation requires those seeking asylum in the EU to assert their claim in the first EU country they enter.

The U.S. has such an agreement with Canada, but Mexico has refused to enter into such a pact. Mexico's refusal, however, in no way prevents the U.S. from enforcing such a requirement under its own immigration law and the discretionary authority granted to the attorney general and the secretary of DHS.

And Mexico does, in fact, have a very generous asylum law, passed in 2011. Indeed, it is broader than the U.S. law. As the Center for Immigration Studies explains, in addition to the U.S. categories of fear of persecution due to race, religion, nationality, membership in a particular social group, or political opinion, Mexico also grants asylum to those who have fled their native countries because they are "threatened by generalized violence, foreign aggression, internal conflicts, massive violations of human rights or other circumstances which have seriously disturbed public order."

This refugee/asylum law, administered by Mexico's Commission for Refugee Assistance, is available to every alien in the caravan. By the way, the law suspends all proceedings to remove or deport any asylum seeker until the commission reaches a final decision in that person's case.

Passing through *another* country without seeking asylum undercuts any claim made upon arrival at the U.S. border. For example, a Honduran who claims he was forced to flee due to political persecution has no compelling reason to go further than Mexico. He obviously has no credible reason to fear he will be persecuted by the Mexican government. Thus, ignoring Mexico's asylum process is *prima facie* evidence that a claim for asylum in the U.S. is bogus.

That is why the Departments of Homeland Security and Justice should use their discretionary authority to categorically refuse asylum to all those in the caravan.

The only reason for these aliens to delay asserting asylum until they reach the U.S. is that they have no credible claim of being persecuted and simply want to get into America for economic or other reasons that don't meet the requirements of U.S. asylum law.

Enforcing this discretionary rule would encourage the Mexican government to return to their native countries all Central and South Americans who illegally enter Mexico on their way to the U.S. Right now, Mexico is not only shifting this problem to the U.S., it is encouraging illegal immigration by accommodating these caravans. There also seems to be involvement by American open border activists according to the Capital Research Center, which points to organizers from Pueblo Sin Fronteras or "People Without Borders" who are "embedded in the caravan."

The U.S. should continue to grant asylum to refugees with legitimate persecution claims. But it must act to stop—before they get into the country and into the administrative hearing process—those who would assert false asylum claims. And that includes everyone in this current migrant caravan.

The Complexities of the Political Ethics of Migration

Rainer Bauböck

Rainer Bauböck is an associate professor at the European University Institute in Italy. His areas of specialization are social and political theory.

I n the political theory debate about open borders and the ethics of immigration control there has been little discussion of trade-offs and a lack of distinctions between admission claims. This paper argues that freedom of movement, global distributive justice and democratic self-government form a trilemma that makes pursuing all three goals through migration policies difficult. It argues also that there are distinct normative grounds for refugee protection, admission of economic migrants and reciprocity-based free movement. Refugees have claims to protection of their fundamental human rights. Economic migrants should be admitted if there is a triple benefit for the receiving country, the country of origin and for themselves. Free movement is based on agreements between states to promote international mobility for their own citizens. These three normative claims call for different policy responses. However, in the current migration across the Mediterranean flows and motives are often mixed and policies of closure by destination states are bound to contribute to such mixing. The paper concludes by suggesting that the European Union as a whole has special responsibilities towards its geographic neighbours that include duties to admit asylum seekers, displaced persons and economic migrants.

[…]

"Mare nostrum: the political ethics of migration in the Mediterranean," by Rainer Bauböck, BioMed Central Ltd., February 8, 2019. https://comparativemigrationstudies. springeropen.com/articles/10.1186/s40878-019-0116-8. Licensed under CC BY 4.0 International.

Three Questions About Immigration Control

In the absence of immigration control, international migration would turn into geographic mobility of the same kind as internal migration within a state territory. Immigration control is thus constitutive of the very phenomenon that we describe and count as international migration. Yet not all potential immigrants have the same claims to be admitted. We can distinguish three broad categories by asking a series of three questions about immigration control.

The first question is whether a state exempts a whole category of migrants from immigration control. By doing so it creates two categories that we may call free movers, for whom international migration is not essentially different from internal mobility, and controlled migrants. Free movement for EU citizens provides the obvious illustration for the former, but similar arrangements exist between Australia and New Zealand and among ECOWAS and MERCOSUR member states. As we will see shortly, however, this category is much broader and has great potential for further expansion.

The second question is whether a state distinguishes further within the category of controlled migrants between those who have individual admission claims and others who don't. Let's call the former entitlement migrants. They include two main types: refugees with a right to asylum and those whom I suggest to call "pre-connected migrants" whose admission claims rely on their special ties to the destination country.

The third and final question distinguishes further within the category of non-entitled migrants by asking whether states have duties to take in certain numbers of immigrants who do not have individual admission claims. I will argue that liberal states should adopt such policies towards displaced persons as well as towards economic migrants.

This leaves a broad residual category of potential migrants towards whom states do not have any positive admission duties. From a liberal perspective this does not entail that states can turn away such would-be immigrants in the same way as the owner of a house may turn away a stranger by simply not answering the doorbell. Liberal democracies derive their legitimacy not only from representing the will of their people, but also from governing according to the rule of law. As pointed out by Schotel, the coercion that states exercise over would-be immigrants through their immigration control qualifies as legally binding for those who are turned away only if these persons have some legal standing. This means that liberal states have to answer when the doorbell rings and provide reasons if they keep the door shut.

[…]

Pre-Connected Migrants and Free Movers

Let me now consider in more detail and in the same order the reasons that would-be immigrants can provide, starting with pre-connected migrants—a category that to some extent cuts across the others.

There is one group of immigrants that all states have to let in without further conditions. These are their own citizens. They are not usually called immigrants, but they do cross an international border, and many have spent years or even all of their lives abroad and may intend to settle for good in the country. Their right to do so is enshrined in international human rights declarations and conventions—e.g. in Art. 13 (1) of the Universal Declaration of Human rights: "Everyone has the right to … return to his country." The UN Human Rights Committee has clarified that the possessive pronoun in "his country" does not only refer to citizens but also to long-term resident foreigners who have a claim to return to places where they have built their lives. They are quasi-citizens even if they have not been granted or have not chosen naturalization. Their claims to return are for this reason similar to those of citizens. The right of the latter to return is furthermore protected by the human right not to be arbitrarily deprived of one's citizenship (UDHR Art. 15 (2)). Today, most liberal states do not consider either long-term residence abroad or voluntary acquisition of another citizenship as a sufficient reason for stripping their nationals of their legal status and right to return.

[...]

One may wonder why, in contrast to a rather weak right to family reunification, the right to return to one's country is one of the few human rights that are not further qualified and seems thus nearly as absolute as the right not to be tortured. The reason is not that returning citizens have stronger needs than families separated by migration, refugees or those who desperately want to improve their economic opportunities. It is instead that states are responsible for their own citizens vis-à-vis other states. Citizenship is a global sorting mechanism that assigns responsibilities for individuals' protection to states. States that fail to readmit their own citizens and to offer them diplomatic protection while they are abroad become in a way 'externally failed states' that do not perform one of the core functions of independent states in their relations to other states.

[...]

Economic Migrants

Economic migration ought to be guided by a goal of pareto-optimal triple wins. If economic migration is beneficial for the host state, the individual migrant and the country of origin, then economic migrants ought to be admitted. This proposition needs to be qualified in several ways.

First, it is not obvious why admitting self-interested migrants for self-interested reasons should be a state duty rather than something that states are at liberty to do or not. The answer to this objection is that we still need to place economic migration within the larger ethical framework under which wealthy democracies have global justice duties towards poorer migrant sending countries and justification duties towards would-be migrants whom they reject. These two normative requirements are sufficient to support an ethical duty to set up mutually beneficial economic migration programmes.

Second, as I have suggested above, destination countries ought to have an economic immigration programme under which certain numbers of migrants can apply for admission. Individual migrants do not necessarily have a personal claim to admission. The reason is that the collective benefits for the receiving and sending country will naturally depend on the numbers and qualifications of people seeking work in the former and diminishing the workforce of the latter.

Third, the triple win rationale applies to first admissions, but not to subsequent decisions about permanent residence or access to citizenship. Having lived and worked in a host state for some years, economic migrants strike roots and acquire individual claims to stay. Moreover, as argued by Walzer democracies cannot legitimately rule over those whom they keep in a position of permanent foreigners.

Fourth, states are primarily responsible for the opportunities and welfare of their own citizens and residents. Furthermore, economic immigration programmes are asymmetrically dominated by destination states, not only because these tend to be more powerful, but also because they must be able to select those whom they are ready to admit to their territory and labour markets. These normative and realist reasons make it more difficult to prevent that migrants are losing out by being exploited and that countries of origin are damaged through brain drain. The triple win criterion suggests thus that economic migration programmes should not be exclusively run by destination states. They require an additional layer of global migration governance, i.e. a set of international legal norms, mediation and supervision by international organisations, and governance bodies in which migrants and sending states are represented next to receiving states.

Fifth, the condition that economic migration should also be beneficial for sending countries does not entail that these have a right to suspend their citizens' freedom of exit in order to prevent an outflow of 'human capital'. The goal must instead be to design economic migration programmes in such a way that the return flow of remittances and qualifications contributes to the economic development of the sending country.

This is a very incomplete list of ethical guidelines for economic migration policies, but it has quite radical implications for Europe. It seems clear that there is a large potential for economically and demographically beneficial immigration from Africa to Europe that could generate a triple win if it were well designed. The current reality is, however, that family reunification and refugee admission are pretty much the only available legal channels for immigration into the EU from Africa, while there is substantial regular economic immigration from other parts of the world that gets little attention. The result of Europe's lack of responsiveness to economic immigration from its Southern neighbourhood is a triple loss. Economic migrants are pushed into the arms of human traffickers, destination countries receive irregular migrants who clog their asylum system and remain blocked from regular labour markets. And countries of origin do not reap many of the benefits in remittances and transnational links to Europe that regular economic migration could yield for them.

Refugees and Displaced Persons

The ethics of refugee admission is very different from that applying to economic migrants. In order to understand what the claims of refugees are, we do not need to stick to the narrow definition provided by the Geneva Refugee Convention that can only be understood in its historical context. The UNHCR's mandate has anyway been extended far beyond this definition. Among political theorists there is a broad consensus that international refugees are persons whose states of citizenship fail to protect their fundamental human rights and for whom asylum granted by other states is the only way of restoring protection in the short run.

The more controversial question is what duties states have towards refugees. As with migration in general, it is useful to start with special duties in order to avoid the misleading idea frequently exploited by populists that each state is expected to be open for all the world's refugees. Just like other migrants, refugees are often "pre-connected" to potential host states and such pre-connections create special responsibilities. If states have contributed to a refugee crisis through supporting an authoritarian regime or selling arms to militias fighting a civil war, they have a remedial responsibility to take in refugees fleeing from such countries. The US did take in a significant share of Indochinese boat people after the end of the Vietnam war, but failed to do so for refugees from Iraq.

The second type of special duty emerges from social connections to potential destination states that refugees have already before departure. Just like other migrants, refugees have claims to family reunification with previously admitted refugees or economic migrants. Since long-term refugees need to build entirely new lives in a host country, this argument extends to broader social and cultural connections that facilitate their integration, such as sharing a language with a particular host society or the presence of an already settled co-ethnic immigrant community there.

The third special duty is positional. Countries that are in a better position to protect refugees have special duties to do so compared to far away ones. Positional duties will generally fall on nearby states and will be proportionate to their capacity to provide protection. Malta may be closer to the North African coast than Italy, but it has fewer capacities.

Current European asylum policies rely heavily on an ethics of positional duties for first countries of asylum with some nods towards special connection duties. There are two obvious problems with this approach. First, it lowers the overall capacity of the international community to provide protection to the level of aggregate capacities of those states that carry special responsibilities for refugees. Second, the distribution of burdens among states is unfair if countries that are closer to a refugee emergency and that have already taken in more refugees from a particular origin in the past are obliged to take in even more.

This unfairness arises as an ethical problem only if we do not think of refugee protection as a purely humanitarian duty. A good swimmer who sees a child drowning near a beach has a moral duty to rescue the child. It would be odd if she refused to rescue a second child or asked others to compensate her for the effort. However, if many people have drowned at this beach, the municipality ought to put lifeguards there who are paid from tax revenues collected from the town's residents.

But why should states that are far away and have not contributed through their own policies to a refugee emergency share responsibilities and burdens with other states? As political theorist Owen has argued, the legitimacy of states' coercive power depends on their capacity to protect fundamental human rights in their territory. If some states fail to do so, all the others acquire a responsibility to provide surrogate protection. Refugee protection is thus, in Owen's word, not just a humanitarian duty; it is a 'legitimacy repair mechanism' in the international state system.

This argument provides support for general duties of states to contribute to international refugee protection. Yet it leaves open two big questions. What can motivate self-interested states to comply with these duties? And what is it that they have to contribute?

The first question conjures up a prisoners' dilemma. States are better off collectively if each contributes a fair share, but they are better off individually if they can pass on the buck to others. Prisoners' dilemmas can often be solved if the same players have to play with each other repeatedly and if they also have to play different kinds of games. Non-cooperative players that dominate one game can then be sanctioned in another one. If they are aware of this, they may play cooperatively from the start. Prisoners' dilemmas can even be avoided altogether if players agree ex ante on coordinating their actions.

The international society of states provides only weak resources for resolving the refugee protection dilemma, but the European Union offers the best possible conditions for doing so. It has institutionalized the necessary coordination mechanisms and its member states play iterated and multiple games in which the potential for punishing, and the incentives for avoiding, non-cooperative behaviour are strong. The EU has thus the institutional capacity for ensuring compliance. Moreover, in the EU context with its internally open borders and joint control of external borders, asylum seekers enter EU territory rather than merely the national territory of a particular member state. Positional responsibilities for refugee emergencies in Europe's neighbourhood apply therefore to the EU as a whole. It follows from these two premises that the EU has special duties to establish a system of fair responsibility sharing among its member states even if no similar system can be established at the global level.

This does not mean that refugees ought to be distributed across EU member states according to a formula measuring integration capacities, such as the one used by the EU Commission's 2015 relocation scheme. Sending refugees to countries where they don't want to go and that don't want to have them is not just bad policy; it is also ethically wrong if the primary goal is to provide effective protection, which includes prospects of integration, to the largest number of refugees. Standards of fairness must apply to member states' contributions to overall refugee protection, not to the numbers of refugees each of them takes in. If a state wants to accept fewer refugees than initially allocated to it in a fair scheme, it ought to pay or transfer other resources to those states that take in more. If these transfers reflect the costs that a preference for keeping out refugees imposes on the refugee admitting states, this should avoid perverse incentives for states that want to be seen as being hostile to refugees in order to shirk their responsibilities. Tradeable refugee quotas combined with a matching mechanism that takes into account non-discriminatory preferences of states for certain refugees and preferences of refugees for certain destinations could provide fair solutions.

This account of duties towards refugees is still incomplete. In the words of Aleinikoff and Zamore, it has an 'exilic bias' that considers only long-term settlement and access to a surrogate citizenship in European states as a solution. For millions of coercively displaced persons, this solution is not adequate. Most lack the financial means and physical fitness required to reach European shores, and many want to stay close to home and return there if and when possible. Betts and Collier have suggested that admitting asylum seekers to European states is wrong because it lures many people into the Mediterranean death trap and diverts attention from the more urgent task of providing protection, jobs and education to millions stranded in refugee camps in the global South.

If the overarching goal is to provide effective protection to the largest numbers of refugees, then it would indeed be wrong to focus only on a fair distribution of responsibilities for asylum seekers among EU member states. We need to acknowledge instead that Europe as a whole has a special positional responsibility for its geographic neighbourhood and must mobilize resources for protecting and providing opportunities for displaced persons in Africa and the Middle East. Such efforts have to be closely synchronized with development policies. In this context, the question of who qualifies as a refugee fades into the background. As pointed out by Aleinikoff and Zamore, the problem that needs to be addressed is massive displacement of people within and across international borders due to wars, failing states and economic or environmental collapse. These are also the 'root causes' that eventually push rather small numbers of refugees and migrants to seek asylum in Europe. Taking them in does not address the causes and does not help those who remain stuck in their region of origin.

Are non-entry policies and the aim to deter asylum seekers from trying to reach European borders and coasts then ethically justified after all? My answer is no for both principled and prudential reasons. The principled one is that refugees have individual rights to protection that have been enshrined in the Refugee Convention and the asylum laws of democratic states. The claims of refugees who have lost the protection of their citizenship of origin resonate with the principles on which democratic states ground their own internal legitimacy. The external function of citizenship as an assignment of responsibility for individuals to states similarly supports a robust individual right to asylum. The prudential reason is that, in the current European political climate, calls for protecting displaced persons outside Europe instead of accepting asylum seekers in Europe provide ammunition to those want to do neither. For populists whose agenda is to close off Europe towards the outside and to dismantle it from the inside, promises to provide assistance to refugees in Africa are just cheap talk that gives them a semblance of respectability.

[…]

Mare Nostrum: An Ethics of Special Responsibilities

I have argued that pre-connected migrants, free movers, economic migrants and refugees have distinct claims that liberal democracies must respond to. Yet this multiple-channels-of-admission approach seems to create a new problem. Aren't these claims competing with each other? And if they are, whom should liberal states let in first or in larger numbers?

From a moral perspective the obvious answer seems to be: those who have the strongest needs. Should Europe then close its doors to economic migrants and its internal borders for mobile EU citizens until it has taken in a sufficient number of asylum seekers and resettled refugees? Something is clearly wrong with this answer. It emerges from two fallacies: the fallacy of measuring incommensurable claims using a single yardstick (of needs) and the fallacy of fixed admission capacities. If Europe stops internal free movement, its member states are likely to be less open for economic migrants and refugees both in terms of economic capacities and political attitudes. And looking around the world which wealthy democracies have taken in more refugees, these often turn out to be the same countries that have run extensive economic immigration programmes. Although it is certainly true at the local level that refugees, economic migrants and less skilled resident workers often compete for the same jobs, at the aggregate level the admission capacity of countries is not a fixed number but tends to expand with their general openness to migration and mobility.

For a political ethics of migration, it follows that states can be expected to honour the different admission claims in their own terms and may be entitled to limit numbers or impose conditions for each category (safe that of returning citizens) where their capacities are exhausted. What they must not do is adding up all immigrants in a single quota and closing their borders once that threshold has been reached.

The second problem that my account raises is how to handle mixed flows and mixed motives if admission claims need to be treated differently. When discussing the ethical principles that ought to guide admission policies I have distinguished refugees, economic migrants and free movers benefiting from interstate agreements. Empirically, these categories are, however, not neatly separate ones but overlap strongly. While I cannot imagine significant overlaps between refugees and free movers, there are very significant ones between refugees and economic migrants, on the one hand, and between the latter and free movers, on the other hand.

This problem goes beyond what a general political ethics of migration can deliver and requires political and administrative skills more than theoretical insights. Yet there is still a general lesson that can be drawn. Destination states themselves enhance the problem of mixed flows through indiscriminate policies of closure that push migrants with different motives and claims towards the remaining small doors of family reunification and asylum, which have not been designed for large flows, or towards the backdoor of irregular entry. If such a policy satisfies the normative criteria outlined in this article it would not reduce migration flows across the Mediterranean. It is also an illusion to believe that the right kind of development policies will reduce outmigration pressure in the short run. They are instead more likely to increase it by endowing more people with material and cognitive resources that enable their mobility before conditions improve opportunities to the point where people can afford to stay. Add to this the demographic discrepancy between the "youth bulge" in the

MENA and African countries and the rapid ageing of European societies. The implication is that Europe faces a choice between accepting many more economic migrants from the South through regular channels and a policy of closure that violates EU values and undermines EU achievements such as open internal borders. The final lesson that I want to emphasize is that context matters for the ethics of migration—not only for explaining the different challenges that countries face because of their history or geographic location, but also normatively, in the sense of special responsibilities for neighbours. The Mediterranean was once the cradle of European civilization. Now it has become a graveyard for many who try to reach European shores. Europe shares a historic responsibility for economic and political crises in the neighbourhood that it colonized in the past. Today, Europe's future depends not only on keeping its internal borders open and defending democratic values against authoritarian governments that have sprung up in its midst, but also on how it responds to migration across the Mediterranean. In fact, these two challenges have become intertwined. 'Mare nostrum' was once an imperial claim. Today it has become an ethical imperative.

CHAPTER 4

Are Countries Culturally Improved by Immigration?

Differing Attitudes Toward Immigration

Carol Tan

Carol Tan is an economist and author of several research papers regarding immigration.

The immigration debate in the United States is driven by unique dynamics — nearly all U.S. residents are descended from immigrants of one kind or another, yet opposition to immigration is anything but rare; the country has a long, hard-to-police southern border that has recently seen an influx of unaccompanied child migrants; and a web of local, state and federal laws make enforcement difficult and can lead to unintended effects.

Attitudes toward immigration have shifted over recent years, but establishing precisely why is not as easy as it might seem. A 2013 metastudy in *Public Opinion Quarterly*, "The Dynamics of Immigration Opinion in the United States, 1992-2012," finds that the effect of national socioeconomic and political events "does not neatly fit conventional wisdom." Indeed, "Economic problems in 1991-92, 2001, and 2008-10 did not increase opposition to immigration, but in the wake of rancorous debates over immigration policy in 1994-96 and 2006-07, and the events of 9/11, opinion on some issues became more negative."

Surveying the state of research, Jens Hainmueller of Stanford and Daniel J. Hopkins of Georgetown synthesize 100 of the most comprehensive studies to date with their own scholarship. Their 2014 paper in the *Annual Review of Political Science*, "Public Attitudes Toward Immigration," investigates the two major scholarly approaches toward the question — "political economy" and "sociopsychological" — to pinpoint the underlying factors that best explain attitudes of U.S.-born residents toward immigrants in

America, Canada and Europe over the past two decades. Political economy approaches are characterized as follows: "Frequently starting from formal models of immigration's economic impacts, this theoretical approach explains immigration attitudes with reference to native-born citizens' individual self-interest." By contrast, sociopsychological inquiries frequently look at cultural responses based on perceived threats to national identity or prejudices generated by local group contact.

The paper's findings are divided into the two categories of scholarship:

Political Economic Approaches Have Consistently Performed Poorly in Explaining the Formation of Native Attitudes Toward Immigrants

- There is little evidence that the effect of migrants on the personal economic situation of natives primarily determines native attitudes toward immigration. A 2011 study by Hainmueller et al. found that "a respondent's labor market position is not a powerful predictor of her immigration attitudes."
- In fact, workers in different segments of the labor market share similar immigration preferences. Workers at all skill levels and industries express more support for high-skilled immigration than low-skilled immigration.
- Natives who are higher skilled are more supportive of all kinds of immigration. When investigating labor market competition in Europe, Hainmueller et al. (2007) found that this relationship holds regardless of immigrant skill level or whether respondents are inside or outside of the labor force.
- Natives employed in growing industries are much more likely to be supportive of immigration. A 2013 study demonstrated this phenomenon by surveying European respondents and examining the impact of sector-level conditions

on the attitudes toward immigration from poorer, non-European countries.

- The perception (or misperception) of the scale of immigration also strongly influences attitudes toward immigrants. A 2007 study and a 2013 study found that opposition to immigration rises with misperceptions about the number of immigrants entering the country.

- Overall, the "labor market competition hypothesis" for explaining anti-immigration attitudes "has repeatedly failed to find empirical support, making it something of a zombie theory."

Sociopsychological Approaches, However, Appear to Find More Reliable Evidence to Explain the Formation of Native Attitudes Toward Immigrants

- Perceived cultural threats are strongly correlated with attitudes on immigration. A 2001 study demonstrated the correlation with such attitudes toward legal and illegal immigration. A 2004 experimental study found that "culturally threatening cues," e.g., immigrants who do not speak the language or are not expected to fit well in the native culture, are more influential in forming attitudes toward immigrants than economic cues.

- Natives with civic conceptions of national identity tend to hold less restrictionist attitudes toward immigration than those who emphasize an ethnic conception of national identity. A 2012 study shows that civic conceptions of identity correlate with less restrictionist attitudes. Deborah Schildkraut's 2005 book *Press "One" for English* shows that "Americans who take an ethnocultural view of national identity … are more supportive of restricting immigration."

- People who hold general negative stereotypes of ethnic groups such as Latinos or Asian Americans tend to be more likely to restrict immigration.

- The level of exposure of natives to immigrants impacts attitudes differently depending on the type and size of immigrant group. A 1998 study showed that white Americans' support for immigration is correlated positively with the size of the documented population, but negatively with the size of the undocumented population. A 2010 study found that white Americans proximity to Asian Americans correlates with less restrictive immigration policies but proximity to Hispanic Americans correlates with more restrictivism, implying that group-specific stereotypes may be activated by proximity.
- A 1996 study, however, showed that the effects of residential proximity depend on the broader political context. The relationship between local demographic changes and immigration attitudes is conditional on the national salience of the immigration issue, which has the potential to emerge suddenly and destabilize existing political alignments. Hainmueller and Hopkins state that "when salient, immigration has the potential to mobilize otherwise left-leaning voters in a right-leaning direction." A 2010 study by Hopkins speaks to these dynamics.

As the research literature review shows, the labor market competition theory — which is frequently used by policymakers to explain why their hands are tied on immigration policy — is not supported by data. "As a political issue, immigration relates to strongly held conceptions of national identity and boundaries, and it has an emotional resonance that many issues do not," the scholars conclude. It is therefore also necessary for further research to provide a more "thorough explanation of how organized groups and political parties mobilize residents on the issue of immigration, and how that mobilization varies across time and space."

Debunking Immigration Myths

Daniel Griswold

Daniel Griswold is a senior research fellow and the director of trade and immigration at the Mercatus Center at George Mason University.

A merica's historical openness to immigration has enriched its culture, expanded economic opportunity, and enhanced its influence in the world. Immigrants complement native-born workers and raise general productivity through innovation and entrepreneurship. Immigrants continue to integrate successfully into American society.

America is a nation of immigrants. That is not a cliché but a simple fact. Almost all Americans today either immigrated themselves or descended from immigrants, whether from England and Germany in the colonial era, Ireland, Eastern Europe, and Scandinavia in the 19th and early 20th centuries, or Latin America and Asia in more recent decades. Today one out of every four people residing in the United States are either first- or second-generation immigrants. Immigration has enriched the United States throughout its history, economically as well as culturally and socially.

Contrary to what some of our leaders and pundits tell us, immigrants strengthen the US economy by filling key jobs in important industries, starting businesses, filing patents, creating new products, and keeping America demographically younger. A large majority of immigrants embrace America's culture of freedom and opportunity. Immigration is both a sign and a source of American dynamism. US immigration policy should move toward welcoming more hard-working immigrants to build a stronger US economy.

"The Benefits of Immigration: Addressing Key Myths," by Daniel Griswold, Mercatus Center at George Mason University, May 23, 2018. Reprinted by permission.

Facts About Immigration

Immigrants come to the United States because of the freedom and opportunity it offers. They come to work and build a better life for themselves and their families. Immigrants fill niches in the labor market, typically at the higher and lower ends of the skill spectrum, where the supply of native-born workers tends to fall short of demand by US employers. Without immigrants our economy would be less productive and dynamic.

- Immigrants boost America's economic growth and raise the general productivity of American workers by providing much-needed skills. Immigrant workers allow important sectors of the economy to expand, attracting investment and creating employment opportunities for native-born Americans. A recent study by the International Monetary Fund concluded, "Immigration significantly increases GDP per capita in advanced economies."
- Immigrants fuel entrepreneurship. Immigrants are more likely to start a business than native-born Americans, whether it's a corner shop or high-tech startup. Among startup companies that were valued at more than $1 billion in 2016, half were founded by immigrants. Among Fortune 500 companies, 40 percent were founded by immigrants or their children.
- Immigrants generate new products, ideas, and innovation. Immigrants make up 17 percent of the US workforce, while filing one-third of the patents and accounting for more than one-third of US workers with a PhD in one of the STEM subjects of science, technology, engineering, and math. One study found, "More than half of the high-skilled technology workers and entrepreneurs in Silicon Valley are foreign born."
- Without immigrants and their children, the United States would soon begin to experience demographic decline. The number of US-born workers with US-born parents is already declining, and will shrink by eight million from 2015 to 2035. Immigrants extend the sustainability of federal retirement

programs by slowing the rise in the ratio of retirees to workers. Without a growing workforce, the US economy would begin to lose its dynamism and leadership role in the global economy.

- Three-quarters of immigrants in the United States reside here legally. The number of unauthorized immigrants has stabilized in recent years at 11 to 12 million. Most illegal immigrants arriving today enter the country legally but then overstay their visas; thus, a wall on the US-Mexican border will not stop most illegal immigration. The most cost-effective policy for reducing illegal immigration remains the expansion of opportunities for legal entry and work.

Five Myths and Realities of Immigration

1. Myth: America Is Being Flooded with Mass Immigration

Reality: The rate of US immigration today is well below its historical average and below that of many other advanced nations.

- According to the Census Bureau, the number of foreign-born residents of the United States was 43.7 million in 2016, or 13.5 percent of the total US population. Although growing in recent decades, the immigrant share of the US population is still below its peak of nearly 15 percent in 1910. In many other developed nations, such as Canada and Australia, the foreign-born are a much higher share of the population than in the United States.

- More importantly, the rate of net migration to the United States today is far below what it has been in previous historical periods. The United States accepts about 1.1 million permanent legal immigrants per year, which is a high number in nominal terms but is historically modest as a share of the US population. The current annual US net migration rate (both legal and illegal, minus emigration), is 3.3 per 1,000 US residents. That is less than half of the US migration rate in the peak years of the Great Atlantic Migration from 1880 to

1910 and below the historical US average since 1820 of 4.3 per 1,000.

2. Myth: Immigrants Depress Wages and Take Jobs from Americans

Reality: There is no evidence that immigrants cause higher unemployment among Americans or depress average wages.

- Immigrants typically complement American workers rather than compete directly with them for jobs. As immigrants supply labor, they also increase demand for housing and other goods and services, creating employment opportunities for native-born workers. This is why, over time, there is no correlation between immigration and the general unemployment rate. In fact, the number of jobs and the size of the workforce tend to grow together.
- For those same reasons, empirical studies have found that immigration has only a small and generally positive impact on average wages. A study cited in the 2017 National Academy of Sciences report on the economic consequences of immigration found that the only native demographic group negatively impacted is adults without a high school diploma. The wage impact on this group is small, in the range of 1 to 2 percent, and the size of this group has declined to less than 10 percent of the working-age population. Evidence also shows that as immigrants move in, native-born Americans tend to stay in school longer and upgrade their education, raising their productivity and wages. For more than 90 percent of American workers, immigration either raises wages or has no impact.

3. Myth: Immigrants Increase the Danger of Crime and Terrorism

Reality: Immigrants are less likely to commit crimes or to be incarcerated than native-born Americans. The risks from immigrant terrorism are relatively low compared to other dangers.

- Immigrants are less prone to crime for a number of reasons. After surveying the available evidence, a major 2015 study on immigrant integration by the National Academy of Sciences concluded, "Far from immigration increasing crime rates, studies demonstrate that immigrants and immigration are associated inversely with crime. Immigrants are less likely than the native born to commit crimes, and neighborhoods with greater concentrations of immigrants have much lower rates of crime and violence than comparable nonimmigrant neighborhoods."

- Foreign-born terrorists have committed deadly attacks on US soil, most tragically on September 11, 2001. But the terrorists responsible for the deaths that day were temporary visitors in the United States on nonimmigrant tourist and student visas. Terrorist acts by permanent immigrants are much less of a theat. According to research by Alex Nowrasteh of the Cato Institute, from 1975 to 2017, ". . . the chance of being murdered in a terrorist attack committed by a chain immigrant or a diversity visa recipient was about 1 in 723 million per year," a risk far lower than death by domestic homicide.

4. Myth: Immigrants Impose a Fiscal Burden on US Taxpayers
Reality: Most immigrants pay more in taxes over their lifetimes than they consume in government benefits.

- Immigrants on average are net contributors to government. Immigrants tend to produce more of a fiscal surplus, or less of a deficit, than similarly educated native-born Americans because they are eligible for fewer government benefit programs. The children of immigrants are also more beneficial for government budgets than the children of native-born Americans because they tend to achieve higher levels of education, earnings, and tax paying.

- Higher-skilled immigrants are especially beneficial to government finances. According to the 2017 National

Academy of Sciences report, an immigrant arriving in the United States at age 25 with a four-year college degree will, over his or her lifetime, pay $514,000 more in taxes than government services consumed (at net present value). An immigrant with an advanced degree will pay a surplus of almost $1 million. Immigrants without a high school diploma impose a lifetime cost on government of $109,000, but the cost is much smaller than that of a native-born adult without a high school diploma.

5. Myth: Immigrants Are No Longer Assimilating into American Culture

Reality: As with immigrant waves before them, today's immigrants and their children are learning English and assimilating into American society.

- Immigrants are acquiring proficiency in English at comparable rates to immigrants in the past. Second- and third-generation immigrants are overwhelmingly fluent in English. As the 2015 National Academy of Sciences report concluded, "Today's immigrants are learning English at the same rate or faster than earlier immigrant waves."
- In other important ways, immigrants are adapting to and integrating into American society. The 2015 National Academy of Sciences report also found that immigrants are more optimistic than native-born Americans about achieving the American Dream. Rates of intermarriage between native-born Americans and immigrants have been rising, including among ethnic and racial minorities.

Cultural Diversity as a Societal Asset

Zachary Woodman

Zachary Woodman is a writer and student at the University of Michigan. His areas of focus include political philosophy and decision theory.

I have spent a couple of posts addressing various spurious economic and fiscal arguments against looser immigration restrictions. But, as pointed out recently, these aren't really the most powerful arguments for immigration restrictions. Most of Donald Trump's anti-immigrant rhetoric revolves around strictly alleged *cultural* costs of immigration. I agree that for all the economic rhetoric used in these debates, it is fear of the culturally unfamiliar that is driving the opposition. However, I still think the tools of economics that are used to address whether immigration negatively impacts wages, welfare, and unemployment can be used to address the question of whether immigrants impact our culture negatively.

One of the greatest fears that conservatives tend to have of immigration is the resulting cultural diversity will cause harmful change in society. The argument goes that the immigrant will bring "their" customs from other countries that might do damage to "our" supposedly superior customs and practices, and the result will be a damage to "our" long-held traditions and institutions that make "our" society "great." These fears include, for example, lower income immigrants causing higher divorce rates spurring disintegration of the family, possible violence coming from cultural differences, or immigrants voting in ways that are not conducive to what conservatives tend to call "the founding principles of the republic." Thanks to this insight, it is argued, we should restrict immigration or at least force prospective immigrants to hop

"Immigration, Cultural Change, and Diversity as a Cultural Discovery Process," by Zachary Woodman, Notes On Liberty, March 1, 2017. Reprinted by permission.

through bureaucracy so they may have training on "our" republican principles before becoming citizens.

There are a number of ways one may address this argument. First, one could point out that immigrants face robust incentives to assimilate into American culture without needing to be forced to by restrictive immigration policies. One of the main reasons why immigrants come to the United States is for better economic opportunity. However, when immigrants are extremely socially distant from much of the native population, there a tendency for natives to trust them less in market exchange. As a result, it is in the best interest of the immigrant to adopt some of the customs of his/her new home in order to reduce the social distance to maximize the number of trades. (A more detailed version of this type of argument, in application to social and cultural differences in anarchy, can be found in Pete Leeson's paper *Social Distance and Self-Enforcing Exchange*.)

The main moral of the story is that peaceable assimilation and social cohesion comes about through non-governmental mechanisms far more easily than is commonly assumed. In other words, "our" cultural values are likely not in as much danger as conservatives would have you think.

Another powerful way of addressing this claim is to ask why should we assume that "our" ways of doing things is any better than the immigrant's home country's practices? Why is it that we should be so resistant to the possibility that culture might change thanks to immigration and cultural diversity?

It is tempting for conservatives to respond that the immigrant is coming here and leaving his/her home, thus obviously there is something "better" about "our" cultural practices. However, to do so is to somewhat oversimplify why people immigrate. Though it might be true that, on net, they anticipate life in their new home to be better and that might largely be because "our" institutions and cultural practices are on net better, it is a composition fallacy to claim that it follows from this that all our institutions are better. There still might be some cultural practices that immigrants would want to keep thanks to his/her subjective value preferences from his or her country, and those practices very well might be a more beneficial. This is not to say our cultural practices are inherently worse, or that they are in every instance equal, just that we have no way of evaluating the relative value of cultural practices *ex ante*.

The lesson here is that we should apply FA Hayek's insights from the knowledge problem to the evolution of cultural practices in much the way conservatives are willing to apply it to immigration. There is no reason to assume that "our" cultural practices are better than foreign ones; they may or may not be, but it is a pretense of knowledge to attempt to use state coercion to centrally plan culture just as it is a pretense of knowledge to attempt to centrally plan economic production.

Instead of viewing immigration as a necessary drain on culture, it may be viewed as a potential means of improving culture through the free exchange of cultural values and practices. In the market, individuals are permitted to experiment with new inventions and methods of production because this innovation and risk can lead to better ways of doing things. Therefore, entrepreneurship is commonly called a "discovery process"; it is how humanity may "discover" newer, more efficient economic production techniques and products.

Why is cosmopolitan diversity not to be thought of as such a discovery process in the realm of culture? Just as competition between firms without barriers to entry brings economic innovation, competition between cultural practices without the barrier to entry of immigration laws may be a means of bettering culture. When thought of in that light, the fact that our cultural traditions may change is not so daunting. Just as there is "creative destruction" of firms in the marketplace, there is creative destruction of cultural practices.

Conservative critics of immigration may object that such cultural diversity may cause society to evolve in negative ways, or else they may object and claim that I am not valuing traditions highly enough. For the first claim, there is an epistemic problem here on how we may know which cultural practices are "better." We may have our opinions, based on micro-level experience, on which cultural practices are better, and we have every right to promote those in non-governmental ways and continue to practice them in our lives. Tolerance for such diversity is what allows the cultural discovery process to happen in the first place. However, there is no reason to assume that our sentiments towards our tradition constitute objective knowledge of cultural practices on the macro-level; on the contrary, the key insight of Hayek is it is a fatal conceit to assume such knowledge.

As Hayek said in his famous essay *Why I'm Not a Conservative*:

> As has often been acknowledged by conservative writers, one of the fundamental traits of the conservative attitude is a fear of change, a timid distrust of the new as such, while the liberal position is based on courage and confidence, on a preparedness to let change run its course even if we cannot predict where it will lead. There would not be much to object to if the conservatives merely disliked too rapid change in institutions and public policy; here the case for caution and slow process is indeed strong. But the conservatives are inclined to use the powers of government to prevent change or to limit its rate to whatever appeals to the more timid mind. In looking forward, they lack the faith in the spontaneous forces of adjustment which makes the liberal accept changes without apprehension, even though he does not know how the necessary adaptations will be brought about. It is, indeed, part of the liberal attitude to assume that, especially in the economic field, the self-regulating forces of the market will somehow bring about the required adjustments to new conditions, although no one can foretell how they will do this in a particular instance.

As for the latter objection that I'm not valuing tradition, what is at the core of disagreement is not the value of traditions. Traditions are highly valuable: they are the cultural culmination of all the tacit knowledge of the extended order of society and have withstood the test of time. The disagreement here is what principles we ought to employ when evaluating how a tradition should evolve. The principle I'm expressing is that when a tradition must be forced on society through state coercion and planning, perhaps it is not worth keeping.

Far from destroying culture, the free mobility of individuals through immigration enables spontaneous order to work in ways which improve culture. Immigration, tolerance, and cultural diversity are vital to a free society because it allows the evolution and discovery of better cultural practices. Individual freedom and communal values are not in opposition to each other, instead the only way to improve communal values is through the free mobility of individuals and voluntary exchange.

Immigration Brings Cultural Capital

Jason Lopata

Jason Lopata writes for Stratfor WorldView. *His topics of focus include globalization and urban development.*

Migration is a hot-button issue around the world, but conversations on the subject may be missing one of its most profound effects. Much of the debate over immigration centers on its economic and cultural implications. Proponents emphasize the labor contribution, new businesses and consumer spending habits immigrants bring to their host countries, while detractors focus on job displacement, remittances and the increased toll on government services. From a cultural perspective, meanwhile, those in favor of immigration tend to argue that immigrants assimilate well to their new countries or enrich the culture with their own. Those opposed, on the other hand, believe that immigrants dilute rather than enhance the local culture.

There is, however, another important (though less direct) aspect of migration that bears considering when discussing the matter. Migrant communities often maintain links with their homelands — through family, friends, and social and cultural networks that reach across borders. In a world where impoverished states are developing in a matter of a few decades, the source of today's "poor, huddled masses" may be the source of tomorrow's investment capital and trade partnerships.

From Developing to Developed

The countries from which great numbers of people emigrate, almost as a rule, are not the kinds of states that have a wealth of capital. Most migrants come from underdeveloped countries — U.S. President Donald Trump recently chose a more colorful

"Immigration and Global Business: Bridging the Culture Gap," by Jason Lopata, Stratfor Enterprises, LLC., January 21, 2018. Reprinted by permission.

phrase to describe them — and make the difficult and disruptive decision to leave their homes in hopes of finding substantially better opportunities abroad. Take the United States' history with immigration. At different times, different immigrant populations have come to the country to escape economic or political hardship in their own home countries. As their countries of origin have grown more prosperous and stable over time, people have stopped leaving them. German and Irish immigrants, for example, flocked to the United States in the 19th century, fleeing poverty and upheaval. Today, Irish and German Americans make up two of the United States' biggest ethnic groups, but few people immigrate to the United States from Germany or Ireland anymore. The same goes for the United Kingdom, Italy and Japan — all countries that once supplied the United States with large immigrant populations.

Though migration patterns have changed over the centuries, the fundamentals of the process have not. Developing countries may not have highly educated workforces, specialized products for export, or bountiful investment capital. But as they rise through the value chain and cultivate their economies, they have more to offer. Some even become important financial centers. Suddenly, connecting to these burgeoning economies becomes advantageous for other states around the world. The countries with the largest immigrant populations from these rising powerhouses will have the best access to them.

Global Tribes

That access can make a world of difference. For as globalized as the modern world is, international business is tricky. Beyond the challenges of distance and divergent legal systems, cultural barriers can get in the way of business between countries. Differences in language and customs are the obvious wrinkles, but the difficulties run far deeper. Much of the business world depends on a system of trust, and research indicates that trust tends to be higher among people of a common culture than it is between people from different backgrounds.

These sorts of challenges aren't necessarily insurmountable. As Ian Morris and I argued in a previous column, many of the people who engage in global business hail from the same English-speaking, Western-educated background, regardless of nationality. Even so, this group by no means encompasses all the world's business leaders. Especially in countries that have recently risen from poverty, the globalized culture of international commerce is still alien to many prominent businesspeople, who connect most easily with others of their own native culture. As people in newly developed countries look to build business and investment links overseas, factors like cultural bonds doubtless play into decisions over where to direct their capital. The presence of a familiar community in a foreign land can go a long way toward fostering international business ties.

Consider the reasons foreign investors would gravitate to a city where many people who share their backgrounds live. For one thing, their cultural ties to the city may inspire an emotional desire to forge commercial links to it. For another, foreign investors could work with people familiar both with their culture and with the city's business scene. And if they needed to visit or relocate to the city, they would find a culturally familiar world awaiting them there.

Capitalizing on Cultural Capital

These factors are the driving force behind some of the biggest trade deals and business links taking place in major U.S. cities today. The presence of large Chinese diaspora communities in places such as New York City and San Francisco, for example, has played a large role in the cities' recent property investment and development booms. Chinese investors and developers, who in many cases want to follow their investments and move away from mainland China, find the culturally familiar communities in these places highly appealing.

The same principle applies for countless other cities and cultures around the world. As a bridge between the cultural worlds of the United States and Latin America, Miami is home to the headquarters of many Latin American businesses. A large Turkish population, likewise, has helped Germany become Turkey's main trade partner. And an international community of Gujarati Indians links diamond industry capitals from Surat, India, to Antwerp, Belgium.

But a recent property development in Los Angeles offers perhaps the clearest example of the strong business connections that immigrants can build between their native and adoptive countries. Last June, the Wilshire Grand Center in downtown Los Angeles — now the tallest tower in the western United States — opened its doors. The company responsible for the venture was Korean Air, whose chairman, Cho Yang Ho, personally oversaw the project's construction down to the last detail, according to the building's architect. Why did Cho take such a personal interest in the project, and why did he choose Los Angeles as its location? The answer lies in his cultural ties to the city.

Cho has a history with Los Angeles, whose metropolitan area is home to the largest ethnic Korean population outside the Korean Peninsula. He earned his Master of Business Administration degree at the University of Southern California, about 3 kilometers (2 miles) from both LA's Koreatown and the Wilshire Grand. (Later on, Cho served on the university's board of trustees and sent all three of his children to the institution; he even hired the school's marching band to play at the Wilshire Grand's concrete pouring ceremony.) In addition to his personal attachment to LA, Cho has important business interests in the city. Korean Air's North American division is headquartered in Los Angeles, which offers the most flights to Korea from any city outside Asia. The Korean cultural and economic infrastructure in Southern California is so strong that LA was a natural choice for Cho in his search for investment opportunities abroad.

Taking the Long View

The Wilshire Grand Center highlights an often-overlooked advantage of immigration. South Korea was a poor, authoritarian country back when so many of its people left it for a new life in the United States. Today it is one of the world's most important countries for business. Los Angeles benefits enormously from the opportunities its large Korean population has afforded it.

When most people think about immigration, they focus on the here and now: How many jobs are immigrants taking or providing? How much money are they costing the welfare state, or how much tax revenue do they generate? These kinds of questions often miss the long-term economic effect of immigration, which has its roots in cultural connectivity. Though the countries most immigrants come from are relatively poor today, they may not stay that way forever. And as their economies develop, the newfound cultural affinities between origin and destination states take on a whole new meaning. Yesterday's immigrants become today's cultural middlemen, funneling investment and trade into their newly adopted countries.

The Problem of Multicultural Identity and Immigration

Bruce Thornton

Bruce Thornton is a research fellow at Stanford University's Hoover Institution.

For people in the United States, immigration has particular resonance. We continually hear that we are a nation of immigrants. Many people see the laws that try to control illegal immigration and its social and economic costs as a repudiation of this heritage—an ethnocentric or even racist attempt to impose and monitor an exclusive notion of American identity and culture. Opponents also charge that these laws invite the police to practice discriminatory racial profiling, creating the possibility that legal immigrants and U.S. citizens will be unjustly detained and questioned.

President Obama stated in 2010 that tough immigration-control laws like Arizona's—which was stripped of several provisions during the most recent Supreme Court term—"threaten to undermine basic notions of fairness that we cherish as Americans." The greater significance of such laws, however, is the way they touch on deeply held and frequently conflicting beliefs about the role of immigration in American history and national identity. These beliefs have generated two popular metaphors: the melting pot and the salad bowl.

Fused into Inclusion and Tolerance

The melting pot metaphor arose in the eighteenth century, sometimes appearing as the smelting pot or crucible, and it described the fusion of various religious sects, nationalities, and ethnic groups into one distinct people: E pluribus unum. In 1782, French immigrant J. Hector St. John de Crevecoeur wrote that in America, "individuals of all nations are melted into a new race of men, whose labors and posterity will one day cause great changes in the world."

A century later, Ralph Waldo Emerson used the melting pot image to describe "the fusing process" that "transforms the English, the German, the Irish emigrant into an American. . . . The individuality of the immigrant, almost even his traits of race and religion, fuse down in the democratic alembic like chips of brass thrown into the melting pot." The phrase gained wider currency in 1908, during the great wave of Slavic, Jewish, and Italian immigration, when Israel Zangwill's play The Melting Pot was produced. In it, a character says with enthusiasm, "America is God's crucible, the great melting-pot where all the races of Europe are melting and re-forming!"

This image, then, communicated the historically exceptional notion of American identity as one formed not by the accidents of blood, sect, or race, but by the unifying beliefs and political ideals enshrined in the Declaration of Independence and the Constitution: the notion of individual, inalienable human rights that transcend group identity. Of course, over the centuries this ideal was violated in American history by racism, ethnocentrism, xenophobia, and other ignorant prejudices. But in time laws and social mores changed, making the United States today the most inclusive and tolerant nation in the world, the destination of choice for millions desiring greater freedom and opportunity.

Of course, this process of assimilation also entailed costs and sacrifice. Having voted with his feet for the superiority of America, the immigrant was required to become American: to learn the language, history, political principles, and civic customs that identified one as an American. This demand was necessarily in conflict with the immigrants' old culture and its values, and, at times, led to a painful loss of old ways and customs. But how immigrants negotiated the conflicts and trade-offs between their new and old identities was up to them. Moreover, they remained free in civil society to celebrate and retain those cultures through fraternal organizations, ethnic festivals, language schools, and religious guilds.

Ultimately, though, they had to make their first loyalty to America and its ideals. If some custom, value, or belief from the old country conflicted with those core American values, then the old way had to be modified or discarded if the immigrant wanted to participate fully in American social, economic, and political life. The immigrant had to adjust. No one expected the majority culture to modify its values to accommodate the immigrant; this would have been impossible, at any rate, because there were so many immigrants from so many lands that it would have fragmented American culture. No matter the costs, assimilation was the only way to forge an unum from so many pluribus.

A Tainted Salad

Starting in the 1960s, however, another vision of American pluralism arose, captured in the metaphor of the salad bowl. Rather than assimilating, different ethnic groups now would coexist in their separate identities like the ingredients in a salad, bound together only by the "dressing" of law and the market. This view expresses the ideology of multiculturalism, which goes far beyond the demand that ethnic differences be acknowledged rather than disparaged.

Long before multiculturalism came along, Americans wrestled with the conflicts and clashes that immigrants experienced. A book from the 1940s on "intercultural education" announced its intent "to help our schools to deal constructively with the problem of intercultural and interracial tensions among our people" and to alleviate "the hurtful discrimination against some of the minority groups which compose our people." One recommendation was to create school curricula that would "help build respect for groups not otherwise sufficiently esteemed." Modern multiculturalism takes that idea but goes much farther, endorsing a species of identity politics predicated on victimization.

Multiculturalism as we know it is not about respecting or celebrating the salad bowl of cultural or ethnic diversity, but about indicting American civilization for its imperial, colonial, xenophobic, and racist sins. Multiculturalism idealizes immigrant cultures and ignores their various dysfunctional practices and values. At the same time, it relentlessly attacks America as a predatory, soulless, exploitative, warmongering villain responsible for all the world's ills.

Worse still, the identity politics at the heart of multiculturalism directly contradict the core assumption of our liberal democracy: the principle of individual and inalienable rights that each of us possess no matter what group or sect we belong to. Multiculturalism confines the individual in the box of his race or culture—the latter often simplistically defined in clichés and stereotypes—and then demands rights and considerations for that group, a special treatment usually based on the assumption that the group has been victimized in the past and so deserves some form of reparations. The immigrant "other" (excluding, of course, immigrants from Europe) is now a privileged victim entitled to public acknowledgement of his victim status and the superiority of his native culture.

For Want of a Shared Destiny

And so the common identity shaped by the Constitution, the English language, and the history, mores, and heroes of America gives way to multifarious, increasingly fragmented micro-identities. But without loyalty to the common core values and ideals upon which national identity is founded, without a commitment to the non-negotiable foundational beliefs that transcend special interests, without the sense of a shared destiny and goals, a nation starts to weaken as its people see no goods beyond their own groups' interests and successes.

Multicultural identity politics worsen the problems of illegal immigration. Many immigrants, legal or otherwise, are now encouraged to celebrate the cultures they have fled and to prefer them to the one that gave them greater freedom and opportunity. Our schools and popular culture reinforce this separatism, encouraging Americans to relate to those outside their identity group not as fellow citizens, but as either rivals for power and influence or oppressors (from whom one is owed reparations in the form of government transfers or preferential policies). The essence of being an American has been reduced to a flabby "tolerance," which in fact masks a profound intolerance and anti-Americanism because the groups that multiculturalism celebrates are defined in terms of their victimization by a sinful America.

No matter how the laws of Arizona and other states fare, this problem of assimilation will remain. Millions of the illegal immigrants in this country are no doubt striving to become Americans despite the obstacles multiculturalism has put in their path. Many others have not developed that sense of American identity, nor have they been compelled, as immigrants were in the past, to acknowledge the civic demands of America and give her their loyalty. Their relation to this country is merely economic or parasitic. Figuring out how to determine which immigrants are which, and what to do with those who prefer not to be Americans, will be the challenge of the years ahead.

Negative Impacts of Immigration in Origin Countries

David Goodhart

David Goodhart is the chair of the think tank Demos and a writer at the Guardian.

In busy offices up and down the land some of Britain's most idealistic young men and women—working in human rights NGOs and immigration law firms—struggle every day to usher into this society as many people as possible from poor countries. They are motivated by the admirable belief that all human lives are equally valuable. And like some of the older 1960s liberal baby boomers, who were reacting against the extreme nationalism of the first half of the 20th century, they seem to feel few national attachments. Indeed, they feel no less a commitment to the welfare of someone in Burundi than they do to a fellow citizen in Birmingham. Perhaps they even feel a greater commitment.

Charity used to begin at home. But the best fast-stream civil servants now want to work in DfID, the international development department. Their idealism is focused more on raising up the global poor or worrying about global warming than on sorting out Britain's social care system.

Many people on the left, indeed many *Guardian* readers, are sympathetic to these global citizen values: they see that the world has become smaller and more interdependent, and feel uneasy about policies that prioritise the interests of British citizens. The progressive assumption seems to be that it is fine to have an attachment to friends and family, and perhaps a neighbourhood or a city—"I'm proud to be a Londoner"—and, of course, to humanity as a whole. But the nation state—especially a once dominant one

"Why the left is wrong about immigration," by David Goodhart, Guardian News and Media Limited. This article first appeared in the *Guardian* Newspaper on March 27, 2013; reproduced here by permission of the author.

like Britain (above all its English core)—is considered something old-fashioned and illiberal, an irrational group attachment that smart people have grown out of.

Intellectual sophistication is, more generally, associated with transcending the local, the everyday, the parochial, and even the national. Replacing the nation with other allegiances seems an attractive, even morally superior, alternative—chiming with globalisation's market freedoms.

We have multiple identities and networks, both local and global, and our rights are protected by international human rights treaties—the nation state, as the political cliche has it, is too big for most of the local things that matter, too small for most of the big international things, such as climate change and nuclear proliferation.

The global citizen worldview also tends to be suspicious of communities. Or rather the idea of community is praised in the abstract but rejected in the particular in favour of a "cruise liner" theory of society in which people come together for a voyage but have no ongoing relationship. This individualistic view of society makes it hard for modern liberals to understand why people object to their communities being changed too rapidly by mass immigration—and what is not understood is easily painted as irrational or racist.

It also explains why this brand of liberalism is unmoved by worries about integration. If society is just a random collection of individuals, what is there to integrate into? In liberal societies, of course, immigrants do not have to completely abandon their own traditions, but there is such a thing as society, and if newcomers do not make some effort to join in it is harder for existing citizens to see them as part of the "imagined community." When that happens it weakens the bonds of solidarity and in the long run erodes the "emotional citizenship" required to sustain welfare states.

Many of my best friends, as they say—in business, academia and the arts—sign up to this global citizen worldview, a sort of mirror image of the strident chauvinism you often hear in rightwing politics and media. But I believe many of these "progressive" beliefs are not only wrong, but are unintentionally damaging to the goals of the social democratic left that many of them pursue.

Large-scale immigration from poor countries to rich is not the best way to achieve a more equal world or to help poor countries to develop. The young idealistic lawyer in the immigration law firm may believe that he or she is doing God's work, or the secular equivalent, but they are usually acting on behalf of a tiny sliver of the global population—the better-off, more mobile people in poor countries who, understandably enough, do not want to wait the several generations it might take for, say, Uganda to become a rich, stable, liberal country such as Britain. The idealistic lawyer is working in the face of the overwhelming opposition of his or her fellow British citizens and against the express wishes of most poor-country governments, who need to hold on to their most dynamic citizens.

Nor is bypassing nation states the route to better global governance. It is true that the world has become smaller and many of its biggest problems can only be solved with international co-operation, but it does not follow that the nation state is therefore powerless and irrelevant. Nations remain the building blocks of international co-operation and only they can bring democratic legitimacy to global governance.

The rhetoric of globalisation, by dwelling on those things that constantly flow across national borders—trade, finance, transport, media, immigrant diasporas—ends up painting a partial picture. (Most of the above are, in any case, still regulated by national laws or international agreements.) It also leaves out areas such as welfare, where the nation state is more enmeshed in people's lives than 50 years ago: think of tax credits. And, in 2008, in that most global of industries—finance—it suddenly became clear that it really matters which national taxpayers stand behind your bank.

Perhaps most important of all, the global citizen worldview misreads just how liberal most rich-nation states such as Britain have become. This is part of a bigger story about western values in the 20th century. In the mid-20th century, political elites in the liberal democratic west began to embrace what the sociologist Geoff Dench has called the "universalist shift"—the belief in the moral equality of all people. This went further than equality before the law and meant that differences of sex, class and, above all, race, were no longer obstacles to someone's full membership in a society. Although the idea did not extend to economic inequality, it was profoundly anti-hierarchical and demanded that power and rewards in society be justified by performance rather than inherited characteristics (such as whiteness or maleness or membership of a propertied class).

This political and legal egalitarianism was not new, but in earlier eras was a largely utopian idea associated with religion (we are all equal in the eyes of God) or radical political movements and Enlightenment philosophers. What brought this idea of moral equality into the mainstream? Two world wars, the Holocaust, anti-colonial movements and the stirrings of the civil rights movement in the US all combined to change human consciousness, at least in the developed world, in the mid-20th century. (Democracy itself was a factor too, with its equality of status within the community of citizens—one person, one vote—establishing itself in most rich countries only in the first part of the 20th century.)

After the publication of the 1948 Universal Declaration of Human Rights, the principle of moral and political equality came to be written into the constitutions and legal systems of all liberal democracies. Along with the American civil rights movement, it prompted, for example, Britain's pioneering anti-race-discrimination legislation of the mid-1960s. The moral and legal equality implied in the universalist shift was not always fully embraced in practice, but it became a standard against which to judge the behaviour of states; it was so used by the 1968-ers against authority in general, and against racism by the leaders of the first, post-colonial, immigrant generation in Britain.

It now seems so banal to believe in the moral equality of all people that we have forgotten what a novel and revolutionary notion it is, and how many people around the world still have traces of more racial and "groupist" worldviews.

All of us in mainstream politics in the developed world now believe in human equality. But too many progressive people have taken the universalist shift a step further—into a challenge to all national borders and loyalties. If all human lives are equally valuable, how can we any longer favour our fellow national citizens over the impoverished masses of the global south? This "post-nationalism" nags away at the conscience of many liberal-minded people.

But it is a category error. It does not follow from a belief in human equality that we have equal *obligations* to everyone on the planet. All people are equal but they are not all equal *to us*. Most people in Britain today accept the idea of human equality, but remain moral particularists and moderate nationalists, believing that we have a hierarchy of obligations starting with our family and rippling out via the nation state to the rest of humanity. Britain spends 25 times more every year on the NHS than on development aid. To most people, even people who think of themselves as internationalists, this represents a perfectly natural reflection of our layered obligations, but to a true universalist it must seem like a crime.

Many people on the left are still transfixed by the historic sins of nationalism. But if people are squeamish about the word "nation" they should use another: citizenship or just society. And the modern law-bound, liberal nation state is hardly a menacing political institution. You join automatically by birth (or by invitation) and an allegiance to the liberal nation state is compatible with being highly critical of the current social order and with support for bodies such as Nato and the EU.

Indeed, the modern nation state is the only institution that can currently offer what liberals, of both right and left, want: government accountability, cross-class and generational solidarity, and a sense of collective identification. As societies become more diverse, we need this glue of a national story more not less. This is ultimately a pragmatic argument. The nation state is not a good in itself, it is just the institutional arrangement that can deliver the democratic, welfare, and psychological outcomes that most people seem to want. It is possible that in the future more global or regional institutions might deliver these things; the EU is one prototype but its current difficulties underline what a slow and stuttering process this is likely to be. (Germany, the least nationalistic of the big European states, was happy to spend about $1tn on unification with east Germany but is very reluctant to spend much smaller sums supporting the southern European economies.)

Anti-nationalists also underestimate just how much the nation state has liberalised in recent decades. One might say that the great achievement of post-1945 politics, in Europe at least, has been to "feminise" the nation state.

The nation was once about defending or taking territory and about organised violence. But now that Britain's participation in a world war is highly improbable, the focus has switched to the internal sharing of resources within the nation – and the traditionally feminine "hearth and home" issues of protecting the young, old, disabled and poor. Notwithstanding recent trimming, Britain's social security budget has increased 40% in just the last 15 years.

The modern nation state has become far more inclusive in recent generations and is underpinned by unprecedented social provision, free to all insiders—but towards the outside world it has become, or is trying to become, more exclusionary. There is nothing perverse or mean-spirited about this. As the value of national citizenship in Britain has risen, so the bureaucracy of border controls has had to grow.

No one knows for sure how many people would come to live in a rich country like Britain if border controls were abolished. But in many poor parts of the world, in Africa in particular, there has been rapid urbanisation without industrialisation or economic growth or job creation. That has created a large surplus of urban labour well connected enough to know about the possibilities of life in the west and with a miserable enough life to want to get there.

Who could say confidently that 5 million or 10 million people would not turn up in the space of a couple of years, especially to a country with the global connections that Britain already has?

The American academic Dani Rodrik plays a game with his economics students, asking them whether they would rather be poor in a rich country or rich in a poor country (where rich and poor refer to the top and bottom 10% of a country's income distribution). Most of them opt for being rich in a poor country. But they are wrong, at least if you just look at incomes. The poor in a rich country are, in fact, three times richer than the rich in a poor country, defined as that top 10% and not just the tiny number of the super-rich. That means our economic fortunes are primarily determined by what country we are born in and not by our position on the income scale. Being born in a country such as Britain, or being able to get here from a poor country, means winning the lottery of life.

It is hardly surprising that so many people are battering on our door to be allowed in. But allowing them in, at least in large numbers, not only creates conflict with poorer people in rich countries but slows down the development of poor countries.

A few countries, such as the Philippines, have become part-dependent on exporting people to rich countries and benefit in many ways from the process. But they are the exception. Most poor countries are actively hostile to permanent emigration. And it is hardly surprising. Desperately poor countries cannot afford to lose their most ambitious and expensively educated people. Phil Woolas, Labour's former immigration minister, recalls a meeting with the Sierra Leone foreign minister in 2008 in which she said: "Your country has just given me £150m to invest in infrastructure, and I am very grateful for that, but the trouble is that 90% of our graduates are in the US or Europe. Can you do anything about that for me?"

Emigration from poor to rich countries is obviously an economic benefit to the individuals and their families—a doctor from Ivory Coast will earn six times more in France, and a Chinese junior lecturer can earn five times more in Australia. And the cost of "brain drain" from poor countries is partly mitigated by the remittances sent home. Annual global remittances are about $160bn—more than twice foreign aid flows and a big chunk of GDP in some countries.

But just as rich countries can become over-dependent on immigration, which then reduces the incentive to improve the training or work ethic of hard-to-employ native citizens, so poorer countries can become over-dependent on emigration, which provides a flow of remittance money but slows the "take-off" to a more productive economy.

There is a particular concern over the importing of skilled health staff by rich countries. Malawi, for example, has lost more than half of its nursing staff to emigration over recent years, leaving just 336 nurses to serve a population of 12 million. Rates of perinatal mortality doubled from 1992 to 2000, a rise that is in part attributed to falling standards of medical care. Excluding Nigeria and South Africa, the average country in sub-Saharan Africa had 6.2 doctors per 100,000 of population in 2004. This compares with 166 in the UK, yet about 31% of doctors practising in the UK come from overseas, many from developing countries.

There is nothing morally objectionable about Britain refusing entry to skilled people from poor countries, or insisting that students or temporary workers from such countries return home after their visas expire. Indeed, if people return to their country of origin after a few years in a rich country it may produce the best outcome of all, a remittance flow followed by the return of a more skilled and worldly citizen eager for change. But this requires a reliable and well-funded immigration bureaucracy in Britain that commands public confidence—something that the UK Border Agency can only aspire to at present.

Rich countries should be saying: we will help you to grow faster and to hold on to your best people through appropriate trade and aid policies; we will also agree not to lure away your most skilled people, so long as you agree to take back your illegal immigrants (which many countries don't). The coalition government's combination of a lower immigration target and its exemption of the aid programme from cuts is an expression of this idea.

Another way in which a mutually beneficial "stay at home" policy might operate is by professional and academic bodies in rich countries encouraging more contact with counterparts in poor ones. Academic and professional exchanges and other forms of networking can help to reduce the isolation that many professionals in poor countries feel.

An asylum system that is too open can also have the unintended consequence of encouraging the most reform-minded people in semi-authoritarian countries to quit rather than stay and fight for change. When the UN Refugee Convention was established in 1951, the Soviet gulag was a reality and the Nazi genocide a recent memory. The convention currently states that anyone is entitled to asylum if they are being persecuted on grounds of "race, religion, nationality, membership of a particular social group or political opinion." As Charles Clarke, the former Labour home secretary, has observed: "These are wide-ranging categories which, depending on your definition of persecution, probably cover hundreds of millions, if not billions, of people living in a world where international communications means that more and more people are aware of their 'rights' and seek to take them up." And human rights case law is gradually widening the definitions.

But many of the largest groups, such as Somalis, applying to enter Britain and other rich countries as refugees are not facing individual persecution but rather are caught up in regional conflicts or civil wars or even natural disasters. They have usually been granted "exceptional leave to remain" or what is now called "humanitarian protection." There is no reason why the leave to remain should be permanent. Civil wars and natural disasters come to an end and countries need rebuilding. Rich countries should try to provide shelter from the storm for people badly affected but then ensure they return to help that rebuilding. As it is, refugees are often dumped in the poor parts of rich western cities where they sometimes live segregated and unhappy lives and can become a long-term welfare burden.

I would guess that 95% of British people think policy should give priority to the interests of national citizens before outsiders should the two conflict, but that does not mean you cannot be an internationalist or think it's a valuable part of our tradition to give a haven to refugees.

A new progressive "stay at home" contract can still appeal to altruistic and charitable instincts in the west, but would work with, and not against, the majority interest in both rich and poor countries. Attracting so many of the world's brightest and best into cities such as London seems an oddly lopsided way of arranging global affairs. Surely it would be in the longer-term interests of rich countries and poor to spread development more evenly.

The bigger point here is the most basic insight of welfare economics. Just as the marginal extra pound is worth more to a poor person than to a rich person, so the educated and ambitious person is worth more to a poor country that has few of them than to a rich country that already has many.

Indeed, mass emigration from poor countries creates a kind of development distortion, the human equivalent of global trade and fiscal imbalances: the best-educated people leave countries that badly need them for rich countries that can certainly benefit from their arrival, but do not need them in any proper sense. Some lucky people end up speeding up the development process for themselves and their families while helping to slow it down for everyone else back home.

What's so idealistic about that?

Organizations to Contact

The editors have compiled the following list of organizations concerned with the issues debated in this book. The descriptions are derived from materials provided by the organizations. All have publications or information available for interested readers. This list was compiled on the date of publication of the present volume; the information provided here may change. Be aware that many organizations take several weeks or longer to respond to inquiries, so allow as much time as possible.

American Civil Liberties Union (ACLU)
125 Broad Street, 18th Floor
New York, NY 10004
phone: (212) 549-2500
email: infoaclu@aclu.org
website: www.aclu.org/issues/immigrants-rights#current

The American Civil Liberties Union (ACLU) is a national organization that works to defend Americans' civil rights as guaranteed in the US Constitution. The ACLU works in courts, legislatures, and communities to defend First Amendment rights, the right to equal protection, the right to due process, and the right to privacy. The ACLU publishes the semiannual newsletter *Civil Liberties Alert*, as well as numerous briefings and reports, including press releases regarding ongoing immigration and asylum news.

Amnesty International
5 Penn Plaza, 16ᵗʰ Floor
New York, NY 10001
phone: (212) 807-8400
website: www.amnestyusa.org

Amnesty International is a global human rights organization that aims to stop human rights violations through research, mobilization, and advocacy. It is dedicated to a number of issues, from protecting refugee rights to ensuring gender and identity equality. Its principles focus on fairness under the law around the world, whether that's related to fair working conditions or freedom of expression. It has several issue-based publications available to read online.

The Cato Institute

1000 Massachusetts Avenue NW
Washington, DC 20001-5403
phone: (202) 842-0200
website: www.cato.org

The Cato Institute is a public policy research organization dedicated to the principles of individual liberty, limited government, free markets, and peace. The Cato Institute aims to provide clear, thoughtful, and independent analysis on vital public policy issues. The institute publishes numerous policy studies, two quarterly journals—*Regulation* and *Cato Journal*—and the bimonthly *Cato Policy Report*. It also has a wide array of articles, commentary, and Cato Studies regarding immigration's impact in the United States.

Center for Constitutional Rights (CCR)

666 Broadway
7th Floor
New York, NY 10012
phone: (212) 614-6464
website: www.ccrjustice.org

The Center for Constitutional Rights (CCR) is a nonprofit legal and educational organization committed to the creative use of law as a positive force for social change. CCR is dedicated to advancing and protecting the rights guaranteed by the United States Constitution and the United Nations Universal Declaration of Human Rights. CCR publishes fact sheets and reports on the topics of constitutional rights, including questionable immigration practices.

Department of Homeland Security
2707 Martin Luther King Jr. Avenue SE
Washington, DC 20528-0525
phone: (202) 272-1200
website: www.dhs.gov/immigration-statistics

The US Department of Homeland Security is the cabinet department charged with public safety in the United States. The department's responsibilities extend from securing national security and fighting terrorism to monitoring immigration. It publishes regular releases with statistics on immigration, refugees, border security, and more. Visit the department's website to find out more regarding immigration law, trends, and statistics.

Immigrant Legal Resource Center (ILRC)
1458 Howard Street
San Francisco, CA 94103
phone: (415) 255-9499
website: www.ilrc.org

The ILRC, born out of a San Francisco immigration help clinic, originated to offer lawyers the resources required to serve immigrant communities. Now the organization has expanded and strives to advance immigrant rights and affect immigration policy. The ILRC works primarily with those in the legal field and conducts training to give immigration advocates and lawyers the tools they need to help their clients. The ILRC issues newsletters and an annual report that can be found on its website.

Immigration and Custom Enforcement (ICE)
ICE Office of Policy
Potomac Center North (PCN)
500 12th Street NW
Washington, DC 20024
website: www.ice.gov

ICE is the office within the US Department of Homeland Security concerned with immigration enforcement and terrorism prevention. It derives its authority from federal statutes. To learn more about its policies regarding everything from international student exchanges to national security, visit its fact sheets online.

Migration Policy Institute (MPI)
1400 16th Street NW
Suite 300
Washington, DC 20036
phone: (202)-266-1940
email: info@migrationpolicy.org
website: www.migrationpolicy.org

The Migration Policy Institute conducts research on current immigration issues and seeks to improve policy and attitudes on immigration. The MPI provides updated, factual information on immigration to the public and policymakers alike. Divided into three branches, the MPI focuses on an international program, a US immigration policy program, and a center for immigrant integration policy. It publishes original research, commentary, articles, and diagrams designed to break down immigration statistics for greater public clarity.

National Immigration Law Center (NILC)
3450 Wilshire Boulevard
#108 – 62
Los Angeles, CA 90010
(213) 639-3900
email: reply@nilc.org
website: www.nilc.org

The National Immigration Law Center is exclusively devoted to fighting for immigrants' rights in the United States. It offers policy counsel and defend rights through educational initiatives and strategic communication. Its main issues include workers' rights, DACA, health care, and education for immigrants, among others. The NILC publishes related materials online as well as monthly updates on current events related to immigration.

UNHCR: The United Nations Refugee Agency
1800 Massachusetts Avenue NW
Suite 500
Washington, DC 20036
phone: (202) 296-5191
email: usawa@unhcr.org
website: www.unhcr.org/en-us/

The United Nations High Commissioner for Refugees emerged after World War II to address the mass displacement of people across borders. Since then it has expanded to aid refugees across the globe. As a subsidiary of the United Nations, the UNHCR monitors and assists in emergencies and works to protect immigrants and end statelessness. For information regarding global immigration patterns and asylum seekers worldwide see its online resources and publications.

Bibliography

Books

Stephen Castles, Hein De Hass, and Mark Miller. *The Age of Migration: International Population Movements in the Modern World*. London, UK: Red Globe Press, 2014.

Aviva Chomsky. *They Take Our Jobs and 20 Other Myths about Immigration*. New York, NY: Houghton Mifflin Harcourt, 2007.

Melvin Delgado. *Sanctuary Cities, Communities, and Organizations: A Nation at a Crossroads*. New York, NY: Oxford University Press, 2018.

Don Gallo. *First Crossing: Stories about Teen Immigrants*. Somerville, MA: Candlewick Press, 2007.

David Gerber. *American Immigration: A Very Short Introduction*. New York, NY: Oxford University Press, 2011.

Juan Gonzalez. *Harvest of Empire: A History of Latinos in America*. New York, NY: Penguin Books, 2011.

Robert Guest. *Borderless Economics: Chinese Sea Turtles, Indian Fridges and the New Fruits of Global Capitalism*. New York, NY: Macmillan, 2011.

Randall Hansen and Demetrios Papademetriou. *Managing Borders in an Increasingly Borderless World*. Washington, DC: Migration Policy Institute, 2013.

Brian Peyton Joyner and Donna Carol Voss. *Deep Dive: Sanctuary Cities*. Lincoln, NE: Golden Rule Omnimedia, 2017.

Mark Krikorian. *The New Case Against Immigration Both Legal and Illegal*. New York, NY: Sentinel HC, 2008.

Valeria Luiselli. *Tell Me How It Ends: An Essay in 40 Questions.* Minneapolis, MN: Coffee Hose Press, 2017.

Marcia Amidon Lusted. *Sanctuary Cities.* New York, NY: Greenhaven Publishing, 2019.

Dina Nayeri. *The Ungrateful Refugee: What Immigrants Never Tell You.* New York, NY: Catapult, 2019.

Mae Ngai. *Impossible Subjects: Illegal Aliens and the Making of Modern America.* Princeton, NJ: Princeton University Press, 2014.

Linda Rabben. *Sanctuary and Asylum: A Social and Political History.* Seattle, WA: University of Washington Press, 2016.

Rinku Sen. *Accidental American Immigration and Citizenship in the World of Globalization.* Oakland, CA: Berrett-Koehler Publishers, 2008.

Eileen Truax. *We Built the Wall: How the US Keeps Out Asylum Seekers from Mexico, Central America, and Beyond.* Brooklyn, NY: Verso, 2018.

Malala Yousafzai. *We Are Displaced: My Journey and Stories from Refugee Girls Around the World.* London, UK: Orion Publishing Co, 2019.

Periodicals and Internet Sources

Megan Alpert, "By the Numbers: The United States of Refugees," *Smithsonian Magazine*, April 2017. https://www .smithsonianmag.com/history/by-numbers-united-states -refugees-180962487.

American Immigration Council, "How the United States Immigration System Works," October 10, 2019. https:// www.americanimmigrationcouncil.org/research/how -united-states-immigration-system-works.

American Immigration Council, "An Overview of US Refugee Law and Policy," June 18, 2019. https://www

.americanimmigrationcouncil.org/research/overview-us
-refugee-law-and-policy.

Michael Clemens, "Economics and Emigration: Million Dollar
Bills on the Sidewalk?" *Journal of Economic Perspectives,*
2011. https://pubs.aeaweb.org/doi/pdfplus/10.1257
/jep.25.3.83.

Claire Felter and Danielle Renwick, "The US Immigration
Debate," Council on Foreign Relations, July 25, 2019,
https://www.cfr.org/backgrounder/us-immigration
-debate-0.

Gallup, "Immigration." https://news.gallup.com/poll/1660
/immigration.aspx.

Jack Herrera, "No One Agrees on the Map of Sanctuary States.
We Made One Anyway," *Pacific Standard,* May 3, 2019.
https://psmag.com/social-justice/no-one-agrees-on-the
-map-of-sanctuary-states-we-made-one-anyway.

Jens Manuel Krogstad, "Key Facts about Refugees to the US,"
Pew Research Center, October 7, 2019. https://www
.pewresearch.org/fact-tank/2019/10/07/key-facts-about
-refugees-to-the-u-s/.

Alex Nowrasteh, "The Case for More Immigration," *Democracy:
A Journal of Ideas,* Fall 2016. https://democracyjournal.org
/magazine/42/the-case-for-more-immigration/.

Jynnah Radford, "Key Findings about US Immigrants," Pew
Research Center, June 17, 2019. https://www.pewresearch
.org/fact-tank/2019/06/17/key-findings-about-u-s
-immigrants/.

Xiaojian Zhao, "Immigration to the United States after 1945,"
Oxford Research Encyclopedias, July 2016. https://oxfordre
.com/americanhistory/view/10.1093/acrefore
/9780199329175.001.0001/acrefore-9780199329175-e-72.

Index